Hilary Ho

Right to the Bitter End

Bitter End

A Survival Guide for Sailing Couples

Adlard Coles Nautical
LONDON

DEDICATION

To Stuart, my favourite sailing companion

Published 1995 by Adlard Coles Nautical
an imprint of A & C Black (Publishers) Ltd
35 Bedford Row, London WC1R 4JH

ISBN 0-7136-4200-9

A CIP catalogue record for this book is
available from the British Library.

Typeset in 10½ on 12pt Italia by
Falcon Oast Graphic Art
Printed and bound in Great Britain by
Cromwell Press, Melksham, Wilts

Contents

Introduction

It never ceases to surprise me that men and women choose to sail together. You would think that with so many other opportunities for sport and relaxation they would find less challenging ways of spending their time; but off they go to their boats, blissfully unaware that they are about to test their relationship to the limits.

They set off so eagerly, with nothing to prepare them for what lies ahead. But how hard it is to keep romantic dreams alive when the boat is heeling violently and waves are thrashing into the cockpit! It saddens me to think of all those carefully prepared candlelit dinners for two that have slipped off the table and crashed on to the floor; and so many intimate conversations that must have been cut short as one of the partners dashes to the side, overcome by a sudden surge of nausea. Countless promising relationships have been ruined by bad weather at sea.

It's not just the weather, either; many couples find that they are simply too close to each other on board. There's nowhere to flee if your partner is annoying you; wherever you turn, there he is. And even if you can't actually feel him pressed against you, he's rarely out of sight.

It's even worse if you've got other people with you. There's just no *room*. You try to mark out your territory by leaving some of your things about, but someone always invades your space, or has the nerve to fall on top of you when the weather's rough. And if you decide on a change of clothes, it is inevitable that all the things you need will be under someone else's bunk, and you will have no choice but to turn their little area upside-down just to retrieve a clean pair of knickers.

These drawbacks are only the most obvious ones. There are many other more subtle irritations, like discovering that you and your partner suddenly don't seem able to communicate any

more. It's not just that he's using new and unfamiliar vocabulary (though this is unsettling enough) – you soon realise that you just don't know *what* it is he wants, and he can't seem to tell you in a language you can understand.

It's no wonder that many couples sailing together find it a dreadful strain – but where can they go for help? When I needed advice I found it very difficult to get the relevant information. I must have looked through dozens of sailing books, and although I could find out how to handle my boat in all conditions, none of them told me how to handle my partner when he seemed to be getting out of control. And what about my overwhelming desire to be warm and comfortable at sea? Was this some type of perversion that I should keep to myself? I searched in vain for the answer.

Then there are those practical problems. How do you keep yourself clean on board? Very few boats have private bathrooms, and it's not easy to wash in a space no bigger than a locker, with only a canvas curtain separating you from your companions. In fact, there is so little privacy on most boats that you might just as well fill a bucket with hot water and sit in it in full view of everybody.

In this book I have tried to address problems like these, using up-to-date scientific research wherever possible, and including practical tips on such important matters as coping with discomfort, communicating with your partner, and keeping fit in confined spaces. There should be something of interest to everyone; and although the book is written from a woman's point of view, men too should enjoy the chance to discuss issues that have been ignored for far too long.

It is only by bringing these problems out into the open that we can hope to prevent some of those tragic 'maritime breakdowns'. If by writing this book I have helped just one sailing couple to survive another season, it will all have been worthwhile.

Hilary Harron
1995

1

• • • • • • • • •

Coping with the Change

There comes a time in the lives of many women when they have to face up to the problem of changing partners. By 'changing partners' I don't mean the female equivalent of wife-swapping (although after a tense couple of days sailing, this might seem an attractive idea); instead, it is the gradual realisation that your partner is not the person he was. At a critical point in the life-cycle of Nautical Man, he undergoes a subtle shift – a kind of metamorphosis, rather like a tadpole when it becomes a frog; but instead of stepping from water to land in a new form, the man changes as he steps aboard his boat, and moves from land to sea. Many women will have noticed this phenomenon, and will be relieved to know that it has at last become the subject of scientific investigation. It is now recognised as a clinical condition, and is known as the Change at Sea.

Although some experts have claimed that its symptoms can be seen in both sexes, the Change at Sea largely affects men. Each individual experiences the Change differently, but careful studies have shown that there are certain tendencies common to all sufferers. So how can you spot the tell-tale signs?

1 Physical changes: Once on board, Sailing Man begins to develop a swagger, or a kind of rolling strut, as he moves about the boat. You will also notice that his voice is deepening too, and becoming considerably louder. You might hear him practising his new vocal range by giving short commands as he paces the deck in an unusually erect manner. Your man might even appear to grow in size – either taller, or broader, or both – but this is in fact an illusion, and discreet observation will show that the man is simply adopting this new posture in order to increase his appearance of authority. If you catch him off his guard, though, you will see he is still the stooped and homely figure that you know so well.

2 Compulsion to explore and mend: This compulsion shows itself as an unaccustomed desire to investigate any mechanical equipment that comes to hand. Even if he has shown no previous interest or skill in this area, your man will suddenly give the impression that he's been doing this for years, and will spend hours at a time consulting manuals. He will scour the boat for things to take apart, and will disappear into its bowels to perform complex operations. He will even (and this can be most painful to watch) attempt to dismantle the engine, although past experience should have taught him that he will never put it back together as it was.

Some experts now think that this compulsion could be explained as showing a primitive desire in the man to mark out his territory. This he does by altering as many objects as he can, and leaving them in significant places around the boat. He is trying to say: 'Look, I did this – this place is mine. See the results of my handiwork, and leave it alone.'

So don't be dismayed if your man seems to be unsuccessful in these mending and exploring exercises; they satisfy a deep emotional need at this particular point in his development – and even if he fails to repair his instruments, at least it keeps him busy.

3 Mood swings and anxiety states: The man going through the Change is subject to moods that can swing dramatically, soaring to dizzying heights, or plunging to the depths of depression. There will be periods of euphoria, usually on Friday evenings, but these can quickly be followed by acute anxiety. Emotional lows are frequently brought on by listening to the weather forecast before setting sail. It's a good idea to monitor your partner's listening habits so that you're prepared in advance for the onset of a depression.

Some women find it useful to keep a daily chart of their partners' mood swings. This helps identify those 'triggers' that can set off unexpected reactions, and can be a valuable aid for those trying to cope with this stressful behaviour.

4 Inflated ego: This symptom of the Change can be most distressing when witnessed by those who are seeing it for the first time, especially when it occurs in someone who is normally reasonable and even-tempered. Once again, it appears to be the physical action of setting foot on board that triggers off the response. Almost at once the ego begins to enlarge, and like a rolling snowball it increases in size as it gathers momentum. His partner can only look on in helpless alarm as the ego expands.

If it reaches vast proportions, the woman finds herself being pushed further and further towards the sides of the boat, and in extreme cases she is forced to jump over the side. When the man's ego becomes as unwieldy as this, it is essential to deflate it. There are several ways to do this, none of them pleasant. The sudden release of pressure almost always results in an enormous rush of hot air, which can send the boat wildly off course.

Those unlucky men who suffer from both swinging moods and an inflated ego will be pleased to hear that medical relief will soon be at hand. Scientists working for the Research Association into Sailing Health (RASH) have developed a course of treatment. This will be known as ERT, or ego reduction therapy, and the tablets can be taken over a period of years, or as long as the symptoms last. ERT will be available on prescription from your local GP.

5 Delusions: All men going through the Change at Sea suffer from delusions to one extent or another. These seem to be brought about by the dislocation that occurs when men are suddenly released from the restraints of home and work. Many men find that the best way to handle this unaccustomed freedom is to retreat into a fantasy world, and assume the characteristics of one of their nautical heroes.

After a lifetime of observation I have concluded that most men will select a character based on the following types: the Naval Officer, the Buccaneer/Adventurer or the Viking Warrior.

Into which category does your partner fall? Read the following brief descriptions, and see if you can place him.

The Naval Officer

He is a gentleman, polite, well-spoken, brave and unassuming. He is usually British, with traditional British values, and he always sets a good example. He is clean-shaven (except in a crisis), likes to wear a hat with gold braid, and has pale and tapering fingers. Examples of this type are John Mills, Kenneth More, Douglas Hurd, Richard Branson and Horatio Hornblower.

The Buccaneer/Adventurer

He is romantic and flamboyant, a dare-devil, debonair, dashing and athletic. He is cunning, unscrupulous but loyal. He favours open-necked shirts, high boots and, if sufficiently hirsute, wears his hair long and curly, and his moustache twirly-whirly. Examples of this type are Stewart Grainger, Errol Flynn, Kenneth Branagh (sometimes), Kevin Costner (occasionally) and possibly Paddy Ashdown. Sadly, the swash-buckling character is not a popular choice of the sailor of today, possibly because most small boats are not suited to extravagant displays of swinging from ropes (swashing) and swordplay (buckling).

The Viking Warrior

This is a type with a very ancient history. It seems to be remarkably dominant and persistent. The Viking Warrior is competitive, enjoys racing, is physical, loud, unshaven, with hairy chest, hairy legs (which are usually exposed below short shorts) and hairy feet exposed below the legs, often with knobbly toes. These types are not renowned for their sensitivity. Examples include Arnold Schwarzenegger, Antony Quinn, Sylvester Stallone, and Wolf of Gladiator fame.

To help you categorise your partner, I have included a 'Dress Your Man' activity. Try to adapt the man doll to remind you of your partner, and then visualise him in the outfit that you think would suit him best. Try to choose the one that you think most closely reflects his character when he is in charge of the boat. Why not encourage your man to make his own selection? Allow him a free hand in this, as the resulting outfit could be revealing. For example, he might choose to wear an ear-ring with his horned helmet, showing him to be an interesting mixture of romance and aggression.

Having discovered the type of nautical character with whom your partner identifies, you now have to decide whether you want to share in his fantasy. What part would you like to play? If he is a buccaneer, try marooning yourself on an island and encourage him to rescue you. You could tie yourself to a tree to make it more exciting. But do take care if you find your partner is a Viking Warrior. Make sure you are fit enough to withstand the excitement; and if you are of a nervous disposition, retreat

4

into a sleeping bag with a lockable zip.

Many women, however, are not able to play along with their partners, nor humour their whims. For them, the Change at Sea can be a particularly trying time. They are unable to look forward to the state of calm that will return as the man steps back on to dry land, and their nerves are stretched taut by the strain of living in a confined space with someone who's not himself.

For these women, help is at hand. There are those who can offer counselling and sympathy, and listen with understanding. One of these is Evelyn Cruise, an 'agony aunt' who, for many years, was a columnist on one of our well-known sailing journals. She has given robust advice to many a downhearted sailing wife, and with her permission I have included a couple of letters from the hundreds she's received on this subject. You might find her replies helpful.

The first letter is from a Mrs A S in Weymouth. She writes: 'Whenever we go sailing, my husband seems to change. He is normally a gentle and considerate man, but on the boat he becomes very aggressive. Instead of speaking normally, he shouts all the time, and gives me orders, instead of asking nicely. It makes me very nervous. I've taken to putting cotton wool in my ears, but I still cringe whenever he comes near me.'

This is Evelyn's reply: 'Your husband is obviously going through the Change at Sea. Try and get him on a course of ERT; this should ease the symptoms, and bring relief to you both. Meanwhile it might help you to know that there are many other women going through the same experience, and you might be able to meet some at your local branch of WIMPS ANON, the newly formed self-help group. [More details of WIMPS ANON can be found in Chapter 3, 'Banging the Drum'.] As well as giving you a chance to talk to others in a similar position, the meetings will help you become more assertive and better able to cope with your husband's ego problem. I'm sending you details, along with a very popular leaflet of mine called *Supporting your Partner through the Change*.'

The second letter comes from Ms F T in Brixham: 'This problem may seem petty to you, but it's really getting on my nerves. As soon as we get on our boat my partner becomes very restless. He roams about the boat, muttering to himself, picking up bits of equipment. Then he spends ages taking them apart, and trying to put them back together again. It doesn't seem to matter

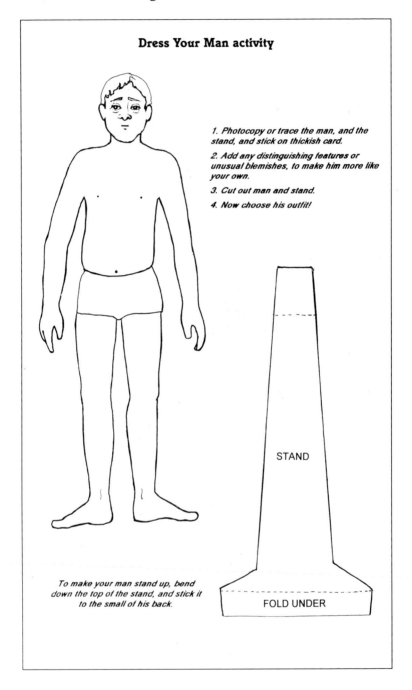

Dress Your Man activity

1. *Photocopy or trace the man, and the stand, and stick on thickish card.*

2. *Add any distinguishing features or unusual blemishes, to make him more like your own.*

3. *Cut out man and stand.*

4. *Now choose his outfit!*

STAND

To make your man stand up, bend down the top of the stand, and stick it to the small of his back.

FOLD UNDER

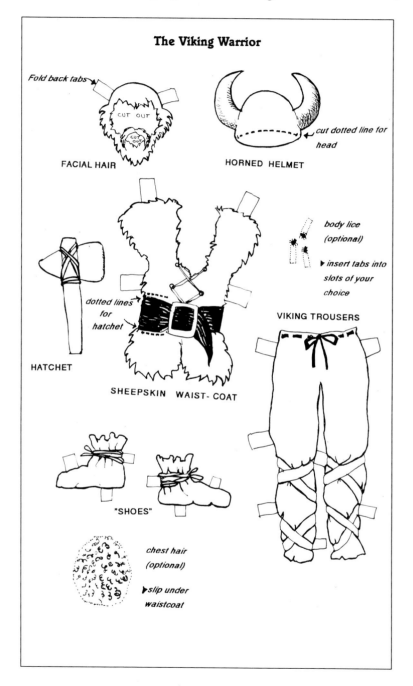

The Viking Warrior

Fold back tabs

CUT OUT

CUT OUT

FACIAL HAIR

cut dotted line for head

HORNED HELMET

body lice (optional)

▶ insert tabs into slots of your choice

VIKING TROUSERS

dotted lines for hatchet

HATCHET

SHEEPSKIN WAIST-COAT

"SHOES"

chest hair (optional)

▶ slip under waistcoat

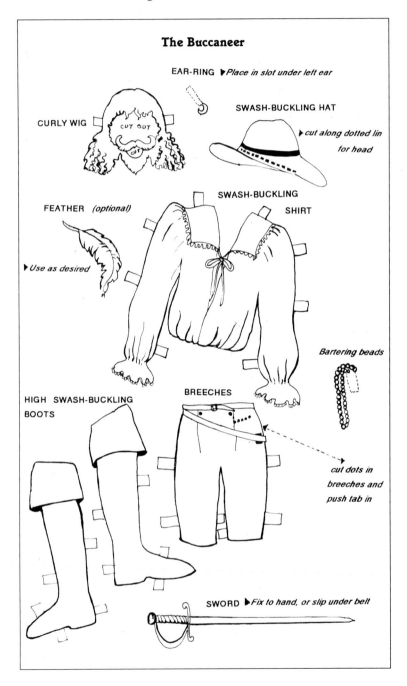

The Buccaneer

EAR-RING ▶*Place in slot under left ear*

CURLY WIG

CUT OUT

CUT

SWASH-BUCKLING HAT

▶*cut along dotted lin*
for head

FEATHER *(optional)*

SWASH-BUCKLING
SHIRT

▶*Use as desired*

Bartering beads

HIGH SWASH-BUCKLING
BOOTS

BREECHES

cut dots in
breeches and
push tab in

SWORD ▶*Fix to hand, or slip under belt*

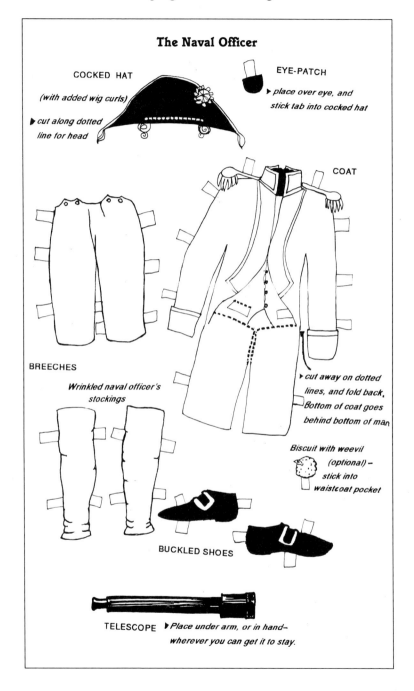

The Naval Officer

COCKED HAT

(with added wig curls)

▶ *cut along dotted line for head*

EYE-PATCH

▶ *place over eye, and stick tab into cocked hat*

COAT

BREECHES

Wrinkled naval officer's stockings

▶ *cut away on dotted lines, and fold back. Bottom of coat goes behind bottom of man*

Biscuit with weevil (optional) – stick into waistcoat pocket

BUCKLED SHOES

TELESCOPE ▶ *Place under arm, or in hand – wherever you can get it to stay.*

whether things need mending or not. He seems to have to investigate their workings. He gets very agitated if I try to stop him, but he's at it for hours. I'm beginning to lose patience, and fear I might do something rash. Please help!'

Evelyn Cruise gives this advice: 'Believe me, you are not the first woman who has had to put up with this sort of behaviour! This compulsive fiddling is all part of the Change. It is thought by the experts to be a necessary male activity, and it really is quite harmless. I'm afraid if you keep trying to stop him he may begin to show unpleasant side-effects, such as feet twitching and finger-sucking. Most women prefer to put up with the fiddling. It *will* get less as the season goes on and the weather improves; when the sun is warm and the winds are light, men seem to be less inclined to investigate their equipment, and more ready to go sailing.'

You will be pleased to hear that both Mrs A S and Ms F T wrote again to Evelyn with encouraging news. Mrs A S learnt much from her local branch of WIMPS ANON. And Ms F T made a bargain with her partner: when they were on the boat together he would try and control his compulsion to explore and mend; but if the need to fiddle became overwhelming, he would return to the boat on his own, where he could indulge in his obsessions to his heart's content.

However, these success stories should not blind us to the fact that there are still numerous couples out there who are struggling to stay on the same boat. It is worth reminding ourselves during these times of near despair that this is only a temporary condition. It will pass, and the pain will ease. Back on dry land, the man will soon return to his usual inoffensive behaviour – the shoulders will stoop once more, and the voice will become soft and questioning again. He will lose his obsession with things mechanical, his ego will shrink back to its normal size, and all will be as it was.

2
· · · · · · · ·

The Comfort Factor

We were beating wearily back to our mooring when our friend, who was at the helm, made a remark that caused me to turn sharply and rip my jogging bottoms.

'Sailing,' he said, 'is, for me, a very sensual experience.' We were all a bit taken aback. Not the sort of view you express in mixed company, I thought primly. Surely sailing is something we do out of a sense of duty? We're not supposed to enjoy it, are we?

My reaction reminded me that we British are still very sensually repressed, particularly when it comes to sailing. We are so used to being uncomfortable on our boats, and cold, stiff and wet, that the closest feeling to pleasure we get is a brief masochistic thrill. Any talk of comfort and sensual pleasure sounds a little decadent.

It is perhaps the men more than the women who have suffered for too long from deep-seated sensual inhibitions. You only have to take a brief look round a boat sailed exclusively by men to realise the extent of their repression. How Spartan and bare it all is! There are no objects to give sensual enjoyment, no pictures, no soft materials, no flowers. And where are the brightly coloured scatter cushions, the crocheted woollen rugs? And is there no tea-cosy, no mat with 'Welcome' on it?

These poor chaps have had the sensuality knocked out of them since boyhood. They have been in the icy grip of the cold shower culture, and the merest glimmer of a sensual glow sends them running for the fire bucket. It's no wonder that they're so much more relaxed when uncomfortable, and so much better than women in putting up with the cold and wet associated with sailing.

Yet surely we shouldn't be ashamed of longing for more sensual pleasure, more comfort, more *self-indulgence* – the kind of

11

cosy warmth that you find by the cottage hearth. Enough of this Spartan austerity, so bleak and unwelcoming. Too many women who step on board, laden down with homely produce, and full of enthusiasm and *joie de vivre*, are put off by the grim conditions of life below decks.

Not long ago, I myself came very close to being put off. I was so sure that sailing was something to be endured that I disregarded the weather forecast, and convinced both my husband and long-suffering friends that it would do us the world of good to go sailing on a crisp day in early spring. However, we miscalculated the tides, and were stuck on our mooring for what seems, in retrospect, to have been several days (though in reality it couldn't have been more than a few hours).

We'd left a small gap in the hatch to let the condensation out; and as we huddled round the stove, my feet gradually lost all sensation, caught in the draught of the bitter north wind that blew through the cabin. We were imprisoned in a cheerless cell; we were even obliged to 'slop out', as our sea-loo couldn't be flushed. Never again! I thought. Never again!

We whiled away the time observing the outside world through a port-hole. In fascination, we watched a fellow in the distance come striding towards us through the mud, wearing thigh-high waders. He was checking moorings exposed by the low tide. As he approached, my friend called out to ask if he'd like a cup of tea, to warm his chilled hands. He called back cheerily, as he passed by, that he'd prefer to keep going – it seemed best to keep moving to stop sinking, he said, and anyway he wanted to finish before the tide came in. As he squelched away, it dawned on us that we too could have walked to the shore. Why hadn't we formed an escape committee? At least one of us would have made it to the land.

Later, back home, snug and warm once more, the others assured me that it had all been a bit of a laugh. But I still can't see the funny side – could it be that I lack a sense of endurance? Some people do seem to be able to tolerate pain and misery much better than others. Do some couples have different discomfort thresholds? Could this be why so many promising sailing partnerships have foundered?

To test this theory, I have devised a questionnaire. It is designed to help you find out how much discomfort you can endure. It will give you a placing on the well-known Macho-

Pansy Scale. Answer the questions as honestly as you can, and when you've completed them you should be able to calculate your Comfort Quotient (CQ). A high CQ means that you need more comfort than you're getting. In fact, it means you are nearer to being a Pansy than a Macho. *This is nothing to be ashamed of.* I myself admit to being a weed, although I have hopes of one day becoming a hardy perennial. Persuade your partner to try it too! You might find you are incompatible:

CQ QUESTIONNAIRE
Tick the answer that most closely represents your view:

1 Would you prefer your boat to have bunk cushions covered with
a wipeable PVC
b dry-cleanable Sanderson's fabric
c removable, washable velour

2 Do you prefer your boat's windows (or port-holes) to have
a Austrian blinds
b nothing
c cotton curtains

3 When your cutlery keeps sliding round the table, do you
a put it back in place
b stick it down with Blu-tack
c eat your food with your fingers

4 How do you feel about cold showers?
a They're manly and bracing
b They can give you a heart attack
c They're all right if you're expecting them

5 What is the longest time you've worn the same pair of socks (approx)?
a Two days
b Two weeks
c Two months

6 Do you enjoy sleeping in confined spaces?
a The tighter the better

What is your preferred method of descent into the main cabin?

b I don't mind
c It gives me claustrophobia

7 In a driving gale, what is your preferred method of descent into the main cabin?
   a Backwards, clinging to the steps
   b Forwards, swinging from the hatch
   c Launching body into space, aiming for nearest bunk

8 Have you fallen off the heads (toilet)?
   a Once
   b Often
   c Nearly

9 Given the choice, would you prefer your clothes to be
   a hanging in a locker
   b under someone else's bunk
   c under your own bunk

10 If you've fallen out of your bunk, how did you feel?
   a It was good fun
   b It gave me a fright
   c I thought it was normal

Preparing to make the tea

11 Do you enjoy ricocheting off solid objects?
   a Not a lot
   b I'm getting better at it
   c Never feel a thing

12 Do you regard a hot water bottle as
   a a necessity
   b a luxury
   c a useful extra water container

13 Do you enjoy being crushed against your fellow sailors?
   a Only if they're attractive
   b Love it – we're all mates together
   c Don't notice it

14 How much personal body space do you need?
   a About 2 cubic feet
   b Whatever my body displaces
   c A cabin of my own, if possible

15 When sailing with unfamiliar crew of the opposite sex, would
   you change

15

a In the heads (toilet)
b In the main cabin
c In your sleeping bag

16 What do you feel about having to put on damp clothing?
a Yukky
b It'll soon dry out
c It's good for you – toughens you up

How flexible are you?

17 Do you find making a cup of tea while the boat is at an angle of 45°
a exhilarating?
b tricky?
c OK as long as you've got your waterproofs on

18 Your ultimate sailing ambition would be
a To go to the States on a luxury liner
b A place on a round-the-world yacht race
c A fortnight exploring the canals of the industrial Midlands

19 How physically flexible are you?
a Fairly elastic
b All right in some positions
c Pretty rigid

20 After being at sea for a week, how long does it take you to stop swaying at the kitchen sink?
a One day
b One week
c One month

Now add up your score, and see how you got on.

SCORES FOR CQ QUESTIONNAIRE

1	*a* 1	*b* 2	*c* 3		**4**	*a* 1	*b* 3	*c* 2
2	*a* 2	*b* 1	*c* 3		**5**	*a* 3	*b* 2	*c* 1
3	*a* 3	*b* 1	*c* 2		**6**	*a* 1	*b* 2	*c* 3

7	*a* 2	*b* 1	*c* 3		14	*a* 1	*b* 2	*c* 3
8	*a* 1	*b* 3	*c* 2		15	*a* 2	*b* 1	*c* 3
9	*a* 3	*b* 1	*c* 2		16	*a* 3	*b* 2	*c* 1
10	*a* 1	*b* 3	*c* 2		17	*a* 1	*b* 3	*c* 2
11	*a* 3	*b* 2	*c* 1		18	*a* 3	*b* 1	*c* 2
12	*a* 3	*b* 2	*c* 1		19	*a* 1	*b* 2	*c* 3
13	*a* 3	*b* 1	*c* 2		20	*a* 1	*b* 2	*c* 3

Add up the total of the answers you ticked, and this will give you your Raw Score. To calculate your Comfort Quotient (CQ), find your Raw Score, divide it by your age, and multiply it by 100. For example, if you are 40 years old, and you scored 32, this is your CQ:

$$\frac{32}{40} \times \frac{100}{1} = 80$$

As a general rule, you should score around 100 to be comfortable for your age.

If your CQ is between **50% and 80%**, you are capable of putting up with a good deal of discomfort. You are tough, resilient and flexible, and are stimulated by gales and hurricanes. You are probably athletic and competitive, and you like your boat to be practical and stripped of all unnecessary fripperies. You don't mind sharing your body space, but you do have a low sensitivity score – so make sure you're not trampling on other people's toes.

If your CQ is between **81% and 130%,** you are prepared to put up with a certain amount of buffeting, but at the same time you like your surroundings to be pleasant and homely. You have learnt to adapt to sudden changes of temperature and shifts of position, and you are able to lean over at quite acute angles. However, you do resent close body contact and could find that the lack of privacy on board makes you a little tense.

If your CQ is **over 130%**, you need to ask yourself whether you shouldn't be hanging up the old deck shoes and taking up something more sedentary. If you are obliged to keep sailing, and money is no object, why not think about changing your old boat for a plush new one? You can have it fitted with as many comforts as you can afford. If your resources are limited, then 'comfortise' your old boat. Have floor-to-cabintop carpeting; install central heating; invest in the latest thermal wear.

What do you do if you find that you have a high CQ, and your partner has a low one? You might be able to come to some compromise, such as making the main cabin your personal space, with luxurious soft furnishings, and plenty of cushions in strategic places to protect you from the worst effects of crashing about below decks. Then you can confine your partner to the more cramped and bare parts of the boat, where he will be better able to appreciate the discomfort.

This questionnaire will have revealed a great range in the size of individual CQs.

Put plenty of cushions in strategic places to protect you when crashing about

Don't worry if yours is higher than you had envisaged – and let no one think less of you because of it. There is absolutely no reason nowadays why you should have to put up with primitive sailing conditions if you don't want to. Always remember the old saying: *a woman who's warm can weather a storm.*

So use some of the tips above to make life easier on board – you never know, your partner might even get to like it!

3
● ● ● ● ● ● ● ● ●

Banging the Drum

When did you first realise that boys and girls were different? I found out at primary school, when the teacher handed out the musical instruments. She always gave the boys the drums, and the girls the triangles. I used to long to be over in the boys' section, where they were tapping out exciting rhythms with their drumsticks; when I looked at my triangle, it seemed a poor limited thing – and however hard I hit it, all I got was a tuneless 'ping'.

And so it's gone on through life. Sometimes I feel I've had enough of playing boring instruments; I want to drop my triangle and make a grab for the drums. And at the end, when I've had my say, how much nobler it will be to go out with a bang rather than a tinkle.

That's why I'm preparing for the Battle of the Drumsticks – for where better to have a skirmish than at sea, where man still reigns supreme. So who will join me in toppling some of those Skippers off their perches? We shan't be too rough, of course; we'll just ease them off gently, one buttock at a time.

But what if our Skippers refuse to budge? Or worse, what if they did give way, and we really had to take over! On second thoughts, I'm not sure I'm ready yet – I think I'm still suffering from that old 'Crew Complex'. What I need is some positive thinking to raise my morale and boost that drooping self-image. In fact, an intensive course of training at WIMPS ANON might be just the thing.

If you haven't heard of this organisation, let me tell you something about it. WIMPS ANON (the initials stand for 'Women in Menial Positions in Sailing') was the brainchild of Eleanor Vang, whose partner was unfortunately lost at sea. After several lonely years of drifting around aimlessly, she returned to England and founded this support group. Eleanor's aim was to help women become more assertive and decisive. Right from the start she resolved that WIMPS ANON would never turn any woman away, even confirmed 'no-hopers' (provided, of course, they could pay the fees).

The organisation also has a hidden agenda: to train the most ambitious of its members to become Skippers. It was Eleanor's dream that one day, perhaps within the next 50 years, some of her reformed WIMPS would be seen skippering around the oceans of the world.

So how does WIMPS ANON work? The first and most important activity for the new member is to recite the WIMPS promise. This bonds the group together, as they stand erect and affirm their pledge: *'Every day in every way I'm growing more like a Skipper'.* All WIMPS are encouraged to repeat this promise at least twice a day, preferably first thing in the morning and at bedtime. Many members are reduced to tears by this emotional event, but once their spirits have rallied they are ready to launch themselves into the varied programme of therapeutic activities. Here are just a few, to give you a taste of how beneficial the group can be:

1 Aversion therapy sessions: To discourage her from being passive, the sufferer is shown a video of a woman in a long flowing dress reclining in a punt, trailing her hand in the water as she is poled along by a handsome young man. As the sufferer watches the video longingly, she is tickled mercilessly on the soles of her feet, or has a cold sponge squeezed down the back of her neck. Other WIMPS members prefer to be given mild electric shocks.

2 Gradual exposure sessions: The sufferer is shown cardboard replicas of things that frighten her, like fearsome-looking Skippers with angry expressions. Sometimes the woman has to be restrained from stamping on the replica, and instead she is prompted to touch it, then speak to it. At first, sufferers may form humble questions or inoffensive statements like, 'Surely it's my turn now', or 'Would you like to make the coffee while I take the helm?' It's surprising how quickly a WIMPS ANON member can grow in confidence.

When these innocuous statements can be uttered naturally and with confidence, WIMPS ANON members can go on to practise commands and more controversial statements to the replica Skipper, like 'Ease the mainsheet – NOW!' 'What *are* you doing

THE WIMP'S PROMISE

*'Every day in every way
I'm growing more like
a Skipper'.*

Creative Swearing

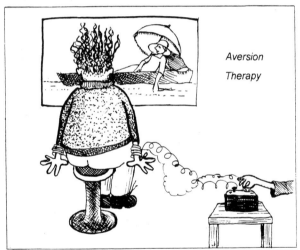

Aversion

Therapy

with that fender?' or 'Do you realise what you did back there?'

3 Role-play exercises: Each member of the group is given a card describing a situation in which a decision has to be made. Some are not very stressful, such as deciding whether to wear tracksuit trousers or jeans; others need more thought – like deciding whether it should be you or your partner who gets marooned on a desert island.

4 Talks from visiting speakers: These are very popular, as they give members a chance to sit down and relax. Many speakers are former WIMPS, and some bring entertaining photographs of themselves and their partners on their boats, trying out their reversed role positions.

The ultimate aim of many WIMPS is to reach the Advanced Class, where the WIMPS strive to become WALLYS (Women at Last Leading Yachtsmen). Here the elite women are trained to become Skippers. For a long time the training was kept secret, but at last we are now beginning to find out just how rigorous the programme is. The recruits are put through a gruelling regime, and as well as having to excel at physical jerks, they have to attend hours of compulsory classes.

One of the most popular subjects is Creative Swearing. In this, they are judged on Imagination and Presentation, as well as colourful Content and Expressive Hand Gestures. Many excel at this, and gain high marks. Others prefer the Story Telling classes, with optional Joking. There are prizes for the most unlikely tale, and for the longest joke – with special credits for those who are also able to remember the punchline.

The final day of the Advanced Class is taken up with a hilarious knock-out competition of Skipper's Bluff. This is the game where numerous mistakes are made; the skill lies in covering them up without anyone noticing. At the end, the one with the fewest 'Guilty' cards is acclaimed Skipper-for-a-day.

Regrettably, all too few WIMPS reach this level. Many find it far too stressful, and realise that they are not yet ready for leadership. But for those who do pass at Advanced level, there is the honour of being presented with the coveted WALLY badge.

This year the badges and certificates were presented by 'Angela' from Brightlingsea. (This is not her real name. WIMPS ANON never reveals the identity of its members.) She thrilled the group members with her inspiring story:

'Before I came to the group I was quite unable to stand up for myself. I was completely dependent on my Skipper. If he got into the dinghy I would panic in case I was going to be left alone; I could do nothing unless he told me. I even had to stay in my bunk till he told me to get up. He controlled everything on board. He rationed the slices of bread, and even measured out water for me to clean my teeth. We were only allowed to use 3 pints of water a day, and he timed the gas from the minute I lit it.

'Once he tried to teach me to row the dinghy, but it wobbled when I got in, and when I let go of the oars he shouted even more. After that he said I was only fit to put the fenders out, and that if I ever touched the helm, he'd cast me adrift.

'Then a friend suggested WIMPS ANON. Since joining them my life has completely changed. I've been able to ask my Skipper to do things, and the other day I touched his helm without permission. When he began to tell me off, I imagined he was one of the pictures in our group therapy sessions, and told him I'd had enough of being told what to do. "So what are you going to do about it?" he taunted. "I'm going to Navigation classes," I said, amazed at my own boldness. "*You!*" he cried. "You've never passed an exam in your life." But I could tell he was impressed. He was quite nice to me after that, and even let me look at his new hand-held compass.

'I finally knew I'd made it when I dropped a pan of beans and was able to swear profusely. I even blamed the pan for having a wobbly handle! My Skipper pretended not to hear, but I could see he was looking at me with a new respect. I smiled to myself as I managed to finish the washing-up in a cupful of cold water. Thank you, WIMPS ANON! No more a WIMP, but soon to be a WALLY!'

Footnote: Since this chapter was written, there has been a move to counter the good work that WIMPS ANON has been doing. An all-male opposition group has been formed: 'Sailing Partners Resisting Attempts to Trivialise Skippering', known as SPRATS. The battle between the two groups has only just begun.

4

• • • • • • • • •

Give Us a Clue

It has often been said that if the good Lord had intended men
and women to sail together, He'd have made them with inbuilt
radio equipment. We all know how difficult it is to have good
communication between the sexes. There are a few fortunate
couples who seem to be on the same wavelength, but the
majority of us seem to spend our time twiddling the knobs, trying in frustration to get through to our partners, and frequently
misunderstanding the messages that come winging back
through the air-waves.

Now it is possible to communicate; it just takes a lot of practice and patience. Before you set foot on board, have a few signalling sessions with your partner. First you must get his
attention: by shouting, or whistling, or gesticulating; and then,
once you've got his attention, try to keep his concentration.
Many women find that their partners have rather poor concentration. If this is the case, maintain eye contact, if at all possible.
You may have to use quite a range of techniques to do this, as
he can easily get distracted. There are many aids you can use
once you are on board, such as torches, flags and balls; but just
use your body to start with, and experiment with gestures,
sounds and facial expressions.

When you think your partner has understood the message,
test him by asking him to repeat it, or set him a practical task,
with a series of instructions, and see if he can carry it out. Once
you are able to send short messages to each other without
ambiguity and stress, you are ready to tackle the much harder
task of communicating at sea. I hope this chapter will give you
some ideas, and encourage you to practise your skills.

First, though, let's look at the subject in more detail. The two
most commonly used forms of communication are *verbal* and
non-verbal communication.

24

One fatal result of poor communication

Verbal communication

One of the best ways to communicate is by using words. We use words most of the time in everyday life, at home and at work. It is unusual on land to mime or to use flags or flashing lights to convey your meaning, although – as I have suggested – you can emphasise your spoken words with a variety of forms of body language.

You can still communicate with words on a boat, but you might not find it as easy as it is at home. One of the problems is that a different language is used on board, and you will first have to master unfamiliar vocabulary. Many sailing people use *Boatspeak*; and until you've learnt a few everyday phrases, you might have difficulty in understanding what is being said to you.

(You will learn more about this nautical language in Chapter 5, 'Brush up Your Boatspeak'.)

Here is a brief dialogue that shows how the use of words, mainly of one syllable, can clarify a simple manoeuvre. No difficult Boatspeak vocabulary is used here.

Locating a buoy
We'll go for that one.
Which one?
See that white one?
No, where?
There – beyond the blue boat.
Which blue boat?
The one next to the white one.
White boat or buoy?
White boat.
That dark blue one?
No – light blue.
Over there, with the washing hung out?
No, the motorboat.
So where's the buoy?
Back there – we've just passed it.

This sort of exchange can go on indefinitely, with the couple circling around for hours. However, as you get more practised you will complete your manoeuvre in a shorter time than this, and with fewer words.

Another problem that frequently arises with verbal communication is the unaccustomed *tone of voice* in which certain things are said. This tone of voice is used for giving commands and instructions; it's usually loud, and abrupt, and many women find it grates on the nerves. It's the same tone of voice used by men trying to teach their wives to drive a car, and it can have the same negative results there.

The practised ear, though, will pick out many shades of meaning in what appears to be a loud and commanding tone. Not all shouting is done in anger, and those who would one day like to be Skippers need to practise using the voice with the volume control set quite high.

Here is another sailing scenario, this time the common problem of picking up a mooring buoy. The man is giving instructions to the woman, who is at the helm. It is written as a

Skipper's monologue. Try to read it with expression, to bring out the appropriate feeling behind the words.

'See the buoy? (*calmly*). I'll point to it. Are you in gear? (*anxiously*). We'll approach it to starboard...no (*patiently*), not on the buoy's starboard side, *our* starboard side. I'll give you a thumbs-up when I've got it. Slowly now (*nervously*), not too fast, NOT TOO FAST!! (*more nervously*). That's it...nearly there (*encouragingly*)...slow down...fine...(*reassuringly*)... slow down...SLOW DOWN!! (*urgently*). I've got it! (*happily*). Cut the engine! (*with authority*). CUT THE ENGINE! (*with alarm*). CUT THE ENGINE!! (*breathlessly, arms lengthening painfully*). Well done (*with relief*). No, I know I didn't give a thumbs-up. I needed both my thumbs to hang on to the line. Tea? (*hopefully*). I'd love a cup (*gratefully*).

Most couples find that over the years they improve their understanding of each other by trial and error, and are able to communicate much better once they have learnt to interpret each other's tones of voice, as well as simplifying their instructions. The final dialogue is spoken by a couple who are mooring alongside a jetty. Try to use a variety of tone and volume; reading it aloud will help you.

A I'll take the helm.
B OK.
A Fenders out?
B *Here we are, I've got the fenders. Off I go.*
A Ready yet?
B *Nearly. I like these soft blue covers on the fenders, don't you?*
A Lovely. Warps in place?
B *Hope so. (Thinks: Must put warps under wires...climb over... hang on...ready to leap...)*
A We're coming in! Jump off!
B *(Thinks: Whoops...seem to be caught on something...) Hang on a minute!*
A JUMP!
B *Got my shorts caught on a stanchion!*
A GIVE ME THE LINE!!
B *It's OK – I'm free now. I'll tie it up here. I'll do a bowline, shall I? How does it go? Does the rabbit go round the tree first, or into the hole?*

A B----r the rabbit! Just get it tied on.

B *I think it goes round the tree...there we are, look, I've done a good one...I think I've torn my shorts, though...can you see if they're ripped? There, down there, where I got them caught. Have a look for me.*

A Help me with this boat first. Just tighten up that line.

B *I don't think I ought to bend over. I'm sure they're torn up the back.*

A **FORGET YOUR B----Y SHORTS!** LET'S GET THIS BOAT SECURE.

B *OK. I'm getting good at these knots...I can almost do them without thinking...I'm sure I've split my shorts, though...I can feel a hole, just there...look. Shan't be able to wear these tomorrow. Oh, you look as if you need a drink.*

SILENCE.

This couple have learnt to communicate quite well, using a combination of English and Boatspeak. But could you guess which of the speakers was the man, and how did you know? Could the same words be spoken by someone of the opposite sex? If not, why not? Read on for the answer.

Speaker A was the man, and B the woman, of course. There are lots of clues – did you notice who was giving the orders, who was expecting an instant response, and could you spot the increase in decibels of the man's voice as the situation developed? There was quite a range, from normal to very loud. You might also have spotted the woman's agility, and her attention to detail, both in her knot-tying and in her concern over the state of her shorts. Could you imagine a man being so particular? Or a woman shouting and swearing like that? It's very useful to spot these differences.

I found the silence at the end very expressive. I wonder what unspoken messages were in the couple's minds?

Non-verbal communication

Unfortunately, this type of message-passing is open to as many misunderstandings as the verbal kind.

Non-verbal communication can include all manner of signalling, as long as you don't speak. You can use various things to help you do this, like torches or flags, but the simplest and

Useful signals

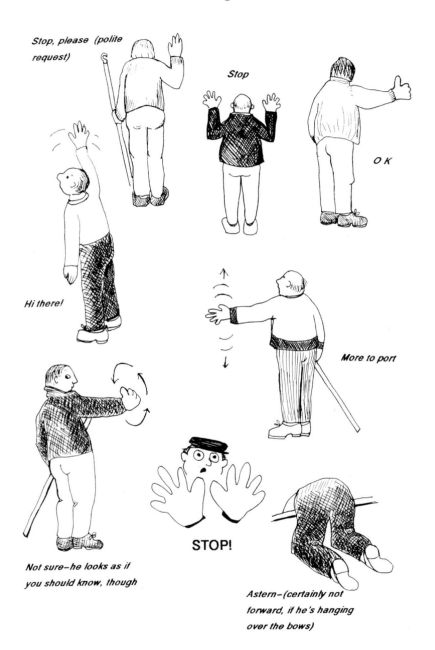

Stop, please (polite request)

Stop

Hi there!

OK

More to port

Not sure—he looks as if you should know, though

STOP!

Astern—(certainly not forward, if he's hanging over the bows)

most readily accessible is your body, used as a whole or in parts.

Much has been written about language, and how we can send signals, sometimes unintentionally, by the way we move, or hold our hands, or change our facial expressions. I must give a word of warning here, though. When you are sailing, try to avoid interpreting your partner's body language unless it is clear that he is making a conscious effort to send out a signal. This is because, on board, the movements of the body are not always under the control of its owner. The body is frequently forced into unnatural cramped positions, or else is hurled into places where it had not intended to go. You cannot presume, for example, if your partner suddenly presses himself against you as you try to peel the potatoes that he is making amorous advances; it is most likely to have been a sudden gust of wind that's tipped him in your direction.

Nor can you hope to get any clues from more subtle signs that his body might be giving you, since its shape is usually concealed beneath layers of clothing, and its natural movements restricted by harnesses, gloves or life-jacket. And if you hope to communicate through facial expressions, remember that the face too can become distorted by factors outside the owner's control; the cold can pinch the features, resulting in frowns and tight lips; winks can be caused by runny eyes, nods by a crick in the neck, and eyebrows drawn upwards by tight fitting headgear. Sea spray can cause the hair to stand on end and stiffen the forehead into anxious lines. Fearsome grimaces can be the result of flatulence or nausea, both common conditions at sea.

Both you and your partner will have to learn to employ more elaborate gestures than you used on land, with whatever parts of the body are most conspicuous. Many couples make their own signalling systems, usually refined over many years. There are some ideas on p. 29 to help you.

But what do you do in the dark, when gestures cannot be seen? How do you pick up a buoy at night, when it's wet and windy, and one of you is sheltered by the coachroof, or you can't hear for the shrieking of the wind, rushing of the waves, and clanking of the rigging?

I have tried various devices to lessen the chance of an accident when we were manoeuvring in the dark. I painted the bobble on my husband's hat with luminous paint, so that I could

Communication Games

A Loaded Message

Um....dot....dot......dash....
Yes...it reads... 'horlicks or cocoa?'

follow his movements; he improved on my invention by rigging up a kind of miner's lamp that he wore on an elastic band around his forehead, powered by a battery in his pocket. However, although it helped him see what he was doing, if he turned his head away I couldn't see him at all. He also found that the wires hindered his movements, and often got caught up on his spectacles.

Then I thought of putting fixed lights on his mittens – red for port and green for starboard. These were quite useful in helping him to put the right mittens on the right hands, but the batteries kept dropping out of his sleeves. There was another snag: I soon realised that if he stood sideways to me, or crossed his hands, I couldn't tell if he was coming or going.

Another idea was to stick a fluorescent strip along his boathook, with a flashing light on the end, so I could see where he was pointing. But nothing seemed foolproof, and there was always the risk that someone would mistake my husband's illuminated boathook for navigation lights. We decided to do our best without the help of artificial aids, rather than lead others astray.

One tried and trusted way of communicating in the dark is by using Morse Code, as long as you have a torch that you can switch on and off. (I knew someone once who used a glowing cigarette end, and by inhaling in long and short puffs was able to transmit brief messages. However, he found it made him feel rather faint.)

Morse Code is not at all easy. Some people find it very hard to tell their dots from their dashes, and this makes it difficult to recognise the words. A friend of mine had exactly this problem. She told me that to improve her sailing skills she'd invested in a course of Morse at her local evening classes centre.

Right from the start she found it difficult to distinguish the letters, but managed to bluff her way through the first couple of lessons. At the third week's class, the instructor announced that he was going to give them a little test to see what they'd learnt. He would tap out groups of four letters, and the class had to write down each word as he did it. He tapped away and my friend listened hard. With increasing alarm she found that each word had the same letters ---S-H-I-T. She looked anxiously around at the others, but they were all scribbling away with no sign of concern. 'It was when everyone read out their words at

Give Us a Clue

The Message Maker

These women have chosen flags from the Message Maker to communicate their feelings. Can you guess their messages?

(The answers are at the bottom of the page.)

DISTRESS SIGNALS

FLAGS OF
DEFIANCE
(MILD)

A. DON'T GO I FORGIVE YOU
B. YOU ARE (AN) OLD CROSS PATCH

the end,' she said, 'that I realised I was on the wrong tack. I made a hasty exit, and joined the macramé class.'

Rather a sad tale, you may think. But fortunately Morse Code is now considered to be rather old-fashioned. There are more up-to-date forms of signalling, and to conclude this chapter I shall mention briefly a recently published book called *The Sailing Couple's Almanac of Signalling Moods and Intentions*, by Deborah Drift. It should prove to be of tremendous help to those who are having problems in the signalling area, as it gives lots of useful tips on preventing misunderstandings at sea.

There are even some new aids to communication given in this book, such as the Patent Mood & Movement Indicator,

Patent Mood & Movement Indicator

BALLS-U-NO

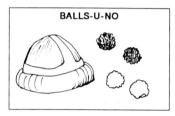

BALLS-U-NO Kit consists of
1 woolly hat with Velcro panels
2 black balls with Velcro patches
2 white balls with Velcro patches

1. BALLS-U-NO

1. One black bobble on top.

Wearer has been at sea for two weeks and is not in command of herself.

Take avoiding action.

2. BALLS-U-NO

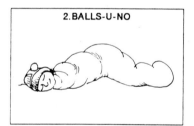

2. One white bobble worn at half hat.

Wearer has taken to her sleeping-bag and is restricted in ability to manoeuvre.

Give a wide berth.

3. BALLS-U-NO

3. One white bobble worn to port

One black bobble worn to starboard.

Wearer extends to at least three feet across—could be wearing wet-weather gear, or have over-eaten.

Avoid impeding her safe passage.

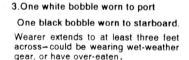

BALLS-U-NO, which should soon be available in all good chandlers. This consists of a hat and a set of detachable woolly balls in black and white, which can be stuck to the hat in various combinations. There is a code to tell you what each set of balls means. This would seem an ideal way to forestall any misunderstandings below decks.

Another aid is based on the traditional use of flags at sea, but it has been revised to make it more relevant to modern sailing conditions. This is called the Message Maker. It is in a boxed set of about 100 most commonly used words, presented as symbols, and printed on flags that can be hoisted in a variety of positions. There is a handbook and cassette with the flags, to help you compose your messages.

I would like to see *The Sailing Couple's Almanac* become required reading for all sailing partnerships as it is so full of useful suggestions and ideas. So when your partner checks that you've got all you need for that weekend cruise, make sure that along with his pilot and Macmillans, he's got your Drift.

5

. . . .

Brush up Your Boatspeak

The boat is another country, so they say; in fact, you only have to step on board to enter the mysterious land of the Nautical folk, with their quaint customs and sailing costumes. Listen, and you will hear them call out in their archaic language, 'Ready about!' 'Ware wash!' 'Fine on the port bow!' These clipped phrases are spoken in 'Boatspeak'. It sounds so tantalisingly familiar, with its smattering of Anglo-Saxon and its strident unmusical tones – not so much Pidgin English as Seagull – that you almost feel you understand what they're saying.

It's the same when you try to read any book on sailing. You can recognise so many of the words, yet somehow they have acquired a new meaning. It can be very frustrating to the new-comer. For example, here is a passage taken from a sailing manual, where what follows is described as a 'typical boat conversation':

Helmsman: There are some nasty waves approaching; watch the speed and get ready to crack the sheets a little.
Mainsail Trimmer: I'm beginning to get too much backwind and I have maximum mast bend and flattener.
Genoa Trimmer: How's that?
Mainsail Trimmer: Better, but I'm still getting too much backwind.
Genoa Trimmer: If the breeze builds any more, we'll have to go to the No 2.

Don't worry if you can't understand what they're talking about. These are the sort of things that Advanced Boatspeakers say. You will find that when you're in Sailing Country, most people can still understand plain English. If you're only in the Elementary Class, you can speak in your own language, but now and again it's useful to try out the odd Boatspeak word.

Now, let's see- the wind's veering to the S E.
I'll tighten the line and let the sheets crack- that new pink one's getting tangled in the prop!...
But watch out!...
Don't like the look of those thermal underpants...
there's been a fair bit of backwind...
I'm going to have to get out that number two...

Confusion can arise in the mind of the beginner, as many Boatspeak words also appear in everyday English.

That way, you will get used to the sound of the new vocabulary.

A typical 'boat conversation' between beginners might go like this:

Skipper (reclining in cockpit): This is the life, eh?

Helmsman/Crew: Yes, it's lovely! You could make a cup of coffee if you like.

Skipper: OK. How about a few more degrees to port? Yes – fine – keep to that course. Do you want a biscuit?

Helmsman/Crew: Not just now, thanks. Where shall we stop for lunch?, *etc*

This conversation, in contrast to the first one, has very little new vocabulary, and would be easily understood by anyone unfamiliar with Boatspeak.

If you are still at this preliminary stage but would like to become more fluent, try learning five new words each day. Write them in a notebook, or on flash cards that you can pin up around the house, on objects, walls, or your partner's back – whatever you see most often during the day. If your partner is still willing to help, he can test you from your notebook, or flash some cards for you. It's surprising how quickly you can build up an extensive vocabulary. Make sure you get the pronunciation right, and use a Nautical tone of voice – you will sound much more convincing to a native speaker if you speak clearly, and with a note of authority.

Before you get disheartened at the thought of that homework, just try the following exercises. It will help you to identify those areas where you have specific weaknesses. You might also be surprised to find that you already know much more than you think! (The answers follow on from the exercises.)

1 Can you think of any Boatspeak words that are the same as parts of the body?

2 Choose the words/phrases that will make Boatspeakish sentences:
a 'What do you think of my neat *bowling/bowline?*' she asked.
b He couldn't stand up because he was hit *on/by* the bumkin.
c He heated up the burgoo and *ate it for his breakfast/used it to stop the leak.*
d She tripped over the *combing/coaming* and fell through the hatch.
e Everyone admired his galligaskins because they were so *wide and strong/thin and long.*
f The skipper shouted so loudly that his voice got *hoarser/hawser* and *hawser/hoarser.*
g As he was fishing from the stern he *caught/got impaled on* a vicious-looking marline spike.
h 'I'd like some puddening,' he said 'to stop the *chafing/hunger pangs.*'
i The shifty-eyed mariner *told/tied* a rogue's yarn to the rest of the crew.
j When the old seaman asked for his daily whack, he got *thumped on the head/given his food rations.*

3 Choose the correct meanings for the following words:
Gudgeon

a a heavy weight on the end of a line
b bad temper
c a metal ring

To hang off
a to hold one rope by another
b to be suspended between the dinghy and the yacht
c to sleep off a hangover

A heeling error
a making the boat lean over unintentionally
b a compass deviation
c wearing the wrong sort of shoes

Gaff jaws
a a piece of equipment for pulling fish out of the water
b losing your false teeth accidentally
c fitting on a spar

Brightwork
a scrubbing the decks
b shiny metal fittings
c cheering up a despondent skipper

Rats tails
a hair after a storm
b what you see before the boat goes down
c sleek ends of ropes

Chafing gear
a it prevents wear and tear
b something that causes ropes to fray
c tight, damp jeans

4 What do the following initials stand for?
a LOA
b LBP
c HWF & C
d BWD & B

5 Read through the following account of an incident at sea, and choose a suitable Boatspeak phrase from the list to put in each space:

'All ----- -- ----!' shouted the Skipper. '---- a --- there, Bob, and ---- --- ----------.' Bob as usual was ----- ------ -- --- ----. He nervously adjusted his --------- ------, and was just -------- --- the ---- ----- jibsheet when the boat ------ and the mainsheet gave him a nasty ----- on the -------. In a ----- -- ------ he was in the -----.

39

Fortunately he was wearing a --- ----, but unexpectedly it ------ -
----. 'Try --------- it!' cried his mates. But too late; he was already
on his way to ---- ----- ------. '------ -- -------!' said the Skipper.
'He's --- --- -------!'

sprang a leak	three sheets to the wind	shiver me timbers
fothering	ease the mainsheet	briny
hands on deck	show a leg	brace of shakes
relieving tackle	cut his painter	buttock
Mae West	Davy Jones' Locker	heeled
smack	starboard	cleating off

6 Have some fun with these anagrams. All these unlikely creatures are hiding the names of things you will find on a boat.

a

PIMPLE BUG

b *RIPPLE ON,
SNAKE*

c

LAW HOUND

d *TECH LAB RAT*

e *I'M A SNAIL*

f *PIG NICKS KART*

7 Which of the three phrases in *a* to *f* on p. 39 is correct Boatspeak?
a by the cringe, bring and buy, full and by
b shifting mood, shifting backstay, shifting sands
c running by the lee, running by the sea, running home for tea
d listing to port, pass the port, pissed as a fart
e stripped to the waist, girded up the loins, stripped to the girt-
line
f round and round the garden, round turn and two half hitches,
hitch your breeches and round we go

8 Can you translate this English passage into Boatspeak? 'See
that rope that's attached to the big sail? Could you make it
looser? Look out! We're going to turn around – the wind is pushing us from behind! Watch out for that large beam of wood – it's
about to hit you on the head! Are you all right, dear? I expect
that gave you a fright.'

So how did you get on with these exercises? You might have
noticed a trick question inserted at one point, just to see if you
were concentrating.
Here are the answers:
1 Parts of the body in Boatspeak are: belly, breast, buttock,
butt (American for 'bottom'), eye, foot, head, heart, heel, knee,
leg, navel (pipe), palm, stern, tackle (slang), throat, thumb,
whiskers.
Score one point for each.
2 *a* bowline; *b* by; *c* ate it for his breakfast; *d* coaming; *e* wide
and strong; *f* hoarser and hoarser; *g* got impaled on; *h* chafing;
i tied; *j* given his food rations.
Score two points for each.
3 Gudgeon: *c*. To hang off: *a*. A heeling error: *b*. Gaff jaws: *c*.
Brightwork: *b*. Rats tails: *c*. Chafing gear: *a*.
Score one point for each correct answer.
4 *a* Length over all; *b* Length between perpendiculars; *c* High
water at full & change of moon; *d* Bath water deep and bubbly.
Score two points for *a*, *b* and *c* – and two points if you managed to think of a good answer for *d*!
5 '*All hands on deck!*' shouted the Skipper. '*Show a leg* there,
Bob, and *ease the mainsheet*.' Bob as usual was *three sheets to
the wind*. He nervously adjusted his *relieving tackle*, and was
just *cleating off* the *starboard* jibsheet when the boat *heeled* and

Practising your Boatspeak

*Alow and aloft there! I must say I **love** the way your knees are bolted on your pinky!*

the mainsheet gave him a nasty *smack* on the *buttock*. In a *brace of shakes* he was in the *briny*. Fortunately he was wearing a *Mae West*, but unexpectedly it *sprung a leak*. 'Try *fothering* it!' cried his mates. But too late; he was already on his way to *Davy Jones' Locker*. '*Shiver me timbers!*' said the Skipper. 'He's *cut his painter!*'

Score one point for each correct word or phrase.

6 *a* bilge pump; *b* spinnaker pole; *c* downhaul; *d* chart table; *e* mainsail; *f* kicking strap.

Score one point for each.

7 *a* full and by; *b* shifting backstay; *c* running by the lee; *d* listing to port; *e* stripped to the girt-line; *f* round turn and two half hitches.

Here are some sample sentences. Each in its own way is inadequate, so perhaps you can improve on them.

a I feel so *full, and by* the way, must we always have beans?

b He's a martyr to his *shifting backstay*; it won't stay rigid.

c She's *running by the lee* again; she really should strengthen those pelvic floor muscles.

d Have you only got one shoe on? You seem to be *listing to port*.

e The Devonshire yokel cried, 'She be *stripped to the girt-line*, the saucy huzzy.'

f Well, you know what they say: '*one round turn and two half hitches* is worth a hundred botched up stitches'.

Score 1 point for each correct answer, and 2 points for each sentence.

8 This is a rough translation – 'Slacken off the mainsail! Look out, we're gybing! Watch out for the boom!'

Note how much more concise the Boatspeak version is, compared to the original English. Also note that there is no equivalent in Boatspeak for the gentle note of concern in the last sentence.

Give yourself a maximum of 10 points for your translation.

Well, how did you do? The most you can score on this test is 105 points, but only native speakers, or those with a higher degree in Boatspeak, could possibly achieve that. A score of 30-50 would be reasonable for a beginner, but if you got less than 30, don't be discouraged. Boatspeak is not the easiest of languages.

So if you don't quite follow what people are saying, just ask them to speak more slowly, and you should be able to get the gist of the conversation. And even if you're still confused, no one will realise if you just smile and try to look intelligent. Practise whenever you can, and with patience and perseverance you will soon be conversing in Boatspeak like a native. Good luck, and don't despair! Or, as we sailors say, '*Haul up your clewgarnets, and all-a-taunt-o!*'

...6...
• • • • • • • •

Dressed All Over

Have you ever been asked to go sailing by your favourite man, and been struck by the thought, 'But I haven't got a thing to wear'? If so, why not take this opportunity to rummage through your nautical wardrobe, throw out the mothballs, and add one or two exciting little items.

After a recent visit to the London Boat Show I was struck by the quantity and variety of sailing wear available nowadays. There seemed to be an outfit for every occasion and for all weathers. But at what a price! Those of us shopping on a budget would find many of these garments far too expensive. Besides, where could we possibly stow them all?

It is a good idea for those with a limited amount of cash to stick to the most versatile items of clothing. One basic outfit can be adapted for wear in many social situations, just by the addition of a few well- chosen accessories. With a couple of garments carefully selected, you can mix 'n' match to achieve the most effective results.

But don't let's forget that our sailing clothes have to be practical as well as smart. With a little care you should be able to be ready for all situations at sea, while retaining that touch of glamour.

The most versatile garment on board must be your little navy outfit. Navy is such a useful colour! Not only does it conceal dirty marks, but also, once you are at sea the blue will co-ordinate beautifully with your legs and ankles, as they quickly turn blue with the cold. Choose from the vast selection of tracksuits in the shops today, or put your own two-piece together, pairing navy trousers with a matching sweater or top.

Once you have chosen your navy two-piece, you will need some accessories. Some ideas for these accessories are given on p. 46.

To complete the ensemble, choose a pair of smart deck shoes

– and why not ring the changes by changing the laces? You can go for a variety of colourways, and co-ordinate with your life-jacket or harness.

If you are still stuck for ideas, have a look at the ensembles on pp. 43–5. A leading sailing magazine recently ran a competition that asked readers to make the best of the few essential items we all have in our lockers. The competition was judged by Betty Ambrose, one of our leading designers of women's nautical gear, and something of a 'fashion guru'.

The long and short of it

Shorts are an essential item to have on board, but which ones to choose? Long shorts or short shorts? They come in such a variety of lengths and widths, and some flatter the legs more than others.

However, it's all too easy to forget, in the excitement of being at sea, that as you move about the boat you are sometimes above eye-level. Try to avoid the embarrassment of accidental exposure. This is more common than you might think, and can happen to both sexes. If you like wearing voluminous shorts, try to avoid climbing up the mast, and scrambling over perspex hatches – unless, of course, you have absolute confidence in your underwear.

Men can also offend by wearing ill-fitting or over-tight shorts. Most women like to be warned in advance before being shown a man's private parts, and an unexpected glimpse can be unnerving, especially at mealtimes. Most people are unaware that their clothing is causing offence. I usually find that a quiet word in the ear is all that is needed – in the same way that it's best to be 'up front' when confronted with unzipped trousers and unbuttoned tops.

Prepared for all weathers!

Now you know how to mix 'n' match, you can now layer 'n' wear! Just start with the thermal undergarments, and add the rest. You might end up looking like Tweedledum, but underneath you'll be as snug as a bug. We have asked our fashion illustrator to draw a cross-section of our model, to show just how she achieved that Tweedle-Dumpty look (p. 49). Beware,

Matching shorts to shapes

Bermudas look well on the leaner figure

Something looser flatters the shorter, fuller figure

Are you a traditional British 'pear'?

An all-in-one jumpsuit might disguise that bottom-heavy shape

though – don't be tempted to wear dungarees under all your other gear if you are likely to need the loo. You have to be a practised escapologist to get out of your waterproof jacket, life-jacket, harness and lifeline in an emergency. It's much better to stick to separate trousers, but remember to peel down *all* the layers before you 'go'!

How to achieve the Tweedle-Dumpty look

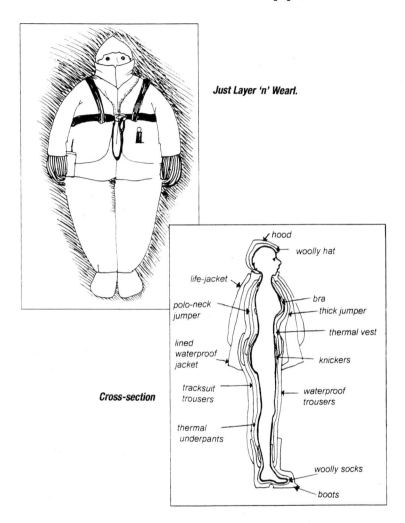

Just Layer 'n' Wear!.

Cross-section

Labels: hood, woolly hat, life-jacket, polo-neck jumper, bra, thick jumper, thermal vest, lined waterproof jacket, knickers, tracksuit trousers, waterproof trousers, thermal underpants, woolly socks, boots

Headwear and hairstyles

We all know how difficult it is to keep looking well-groomed on board. Everything conspires against us – the wind, the rain, the lack of washing facilities; and in the end, all we can manage with our hair is some sort of damage-limitation exercise. But don't be tempted to cut your hair all off, however out of control it may

47

Hairstyles

Try the windswept look. It goes so well with a red nose and blue lips

Crew Cut—a bit butch, but practical

Wet wet wet!

Accentuate a shapely face with clinging rats tails

Nautical styles for long hair

Headwear

A head-band can be so flattering!

A skipper's cap gives an air of authority

The sporty yachting cap— so useful for tucking things in

Life-belt hat for the over-cautious

be. Have it cut short or closely cropped, or choose a style that won't look out of place in a gale, as long as you keep something on top.

We do need a certain amount of hairy covering for protection, not just against the elements – but also to cushion our heads from the blows that frequently occur from parts of the boat that you meet at forehead level. Bald-headed men have a particular problem in this area, and should always wear hats. For many hardy souls, the risk of cracking your skull against a piece of wood is one of the things that makes sailing so exciting – but we don't all need that kind of stimulation.

There is a great selection of hats and caps available in the shops nowadays. Choose one that is tight-fitting if you can, for otherwise it is very likely to blow off, or else be caught in the rigging. Of course you can always fasten it on with elastic, or with hair-grips, but this can be uncomfortable – as well as looking untidy.

Here are a few ideas for hairstyles and headwear. Choose one that suits your hair type and length, but don't be afraid to experiment. It's surprising how a new hairstyle or hat can give you confidence, and the chance to project a whole new image!

Most of us like the excuse to turn out our lockers, and to revamp those tired old outfits. It does us good to buy something new too, even if it's only a small accessory. However, there are some who think that choosing the appropriate clothing is too much of a chore. These are individuals of a robust disposition, who have decided that it's not necessary to wear anything at all. They would certainly pooh-pooh my calls for modest attire. They don't care a fig-leaf for revealing private parts, and being improperly zipped and buttoned just leaves them cold. These are the nature-loving people who are happy with their bodies, and are pleased to display them to all and sundry.

So why *not* discard all your clothing? What have you got to hide? Far be it from me to be a killjoy, but I can foresee a few unhappy consequences. You could get snagged in the rigging on board, particularly on the projecting parts. You could also get very cold, especially in the Outer Hebrides. But if your desire is to go 'skinny-sailing', then who am I to pour cold water on it?

How to make the most of a limited wardrobe.

We asked sailing women from all over the country to combine some of the basic garments in original and eye-catching ways. The best ideas were chosen by Betty Ambrose, and the winners were asked to model their outfits. Betty added her comments.

The basics.

thermal underwear

swimsuit

deck shoes

underwear

T-shirt

1 large scarf

shorts

navy two-piece

hat, boots, socks

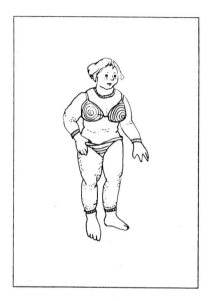

Lotte, from Totnes

'Lotte', says Betty, 'has obviously been inspired by Vivian Westwood. She has chosen to wear her bra and pants (or is it her bikini?) over her thermal underwear. Witty and amusing combination.'

Celia from Deal

Betty comments: 'I love the childish Shirley Temple look! Celia has teamed shorts with deck boots. The hooped shapes in the legs of the shorts and the tops of the boots give an airy, umbrella-like effect.'

Margaret from Scarborough

'You really need a figure like Margaret's to get away with this casual look,' says Betty. 'A clever combination of scarf and T-shirt, topped off by a jaunty hat, all make for a youthful and aggressive appeal.'

Brian from Cowes

We didn't expect any men to enter our competition, but Brian says he has always enjoyed designing his own clothes. 'I particularly like the choice of tartan to co-ordinate the outfit,' says Betty. 'And although his accessories are a little on the small side, they are most attractively arranged.'

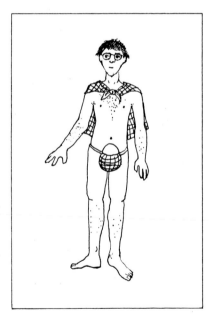

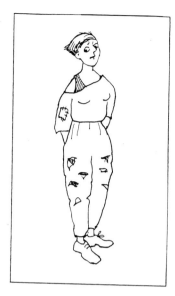

Lizzie from Grimsby

has just the answer if you suffer from the damp. She has cut holes in her two piece- not just for appearance, but for ventilation. 'Wet bottoms can certainly be a problem on board', says Betty. 'Lizzie has managed to put together an outfit that is both practical and stylish. She certainly looks fashionably distressed.'

Conchita from Poole

Conchita admits she cheated by borrowing a friend's cap to make the bra-top but is very pleased with the result. Betty comments: 'What an exotic outfit! A great success. But how about a bunch of grapes and a pineapple on the turban to complete that Carmen Miranda look?'

53

How to look your best at sea

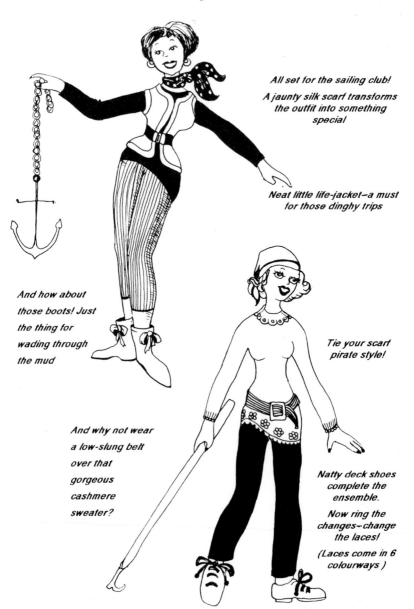

All set for the sailing club!

A jaunty silk scarf transforms the outfit into something special

Neat little life-jacket–a must for those dinghy trips

And how about those boots! Just the thing for wading through the mud

Tie your scarf pirate style!

And why not wear a low-slung belt over that gorgeous cashmere sweater?

Natty deck shoes complete the ensemble.

Now ring the changes–change the laces!

(Laces come in 6 colourways)

7

•••••••••

Shipshape and Bristol Fashion

After a few days on board you might begin to notice that things are not as clean as you'd like them to be. Clothes are damp and don't have that spring-fresh smell, hair loses its shine, and bodies get dusty. Now is the time to give yourself a good wash down, to get rid of all that salt and accumulated debris that gets lodged in the body's crevices. Once the barnacles have been scraped off the bottom, the scuppers flushed and the poop scrubbed clean, everything – both you and the boat – should be in proper seamanlike order.

In this chapter we shall be thinking about the problems of washing and freshening up people on board, and also considering different ways of keeping in trim. We sailors have to keep our bodies shipshape too, and repair our damaged parts so that we can run efficiently.

It has been a source of concern to me that although sailing is a sport, it doesn't keep me fit. In fact, I often find I've put on weight after a few days at sea. I used to think this was because my body had absorbed some of the dampness in the air; later, I reasoned that perhaps the pull of gravity was stronger on land than it was on the sea, so that I only *appeared* to weigh more when I stepped ashore. But now I am better informed; I realise I put on weight because I eat more when I'm on the boat, and exercise less.

That is strange, you may think: to exercise *less*? Surely I must be hauling on the sheets, snatching up buoys, and hurling fenders about? Sadly, this is not the case. I seem to be stuck with the sedentary activities, like helming, and the odd spot of navigation. It's my husband who is constantly exerting himself physically. As a result, he keeps fit and trim, enjoys his food, and sleeps well at night; while I enjoy my food, expand quietly, and am rather fidgety at night.

This is not the place to dwell on my problems, but I must admit to having difficulty confining my legs to the sleeping bag. They seem to want to wander off and explore on their own. I have heard recently that this is a recognised medical condition, and is known as 'restless leg syndrome'. It has no clear-cut cause, but in my case, as it is more apparent when I'm on board, I attribute it to lack of exercise. My legs are trying to make up in the night for their lack of use during the day. 'We want to run about,' they're trying to tell me. But since the rest of the body refuses to co-operate, eventually the legs fall into line and get back in the bag.

For those of us who suffer from restless legs, slipping waistlines, running noses and wandering eyes, I have tried to devise various forms of exercise, if only to keep things in their proper place. Of course, if you've had a chance to row the dinghy about (see Chapter 9, 'The Tender Trap'), or have been allowed to shin up the mast (see Chapter 8, 'Oneupwomanship'), you will have had enough exercise for one day. If not, you will need to be more inventive.

There is no reason why land-based sports should not be adapted to the boat. However, the one major problem is lack of space; you are bound to find that the size of your cockpit hampers your movements. Nevertheless, it is still possible for many activities that usually need a long run, or a big area, to be done on the spot. Here are some examples:

1 Running or jogging: You can run or jog in quite a small space, if you do it on the spot, and it's very good for increasing the heart rate and keeping knees supple. If, however, you are grossly overweight, it might be a mistake to pound the deck in a confined area for any length of time – and it will probably make you very unpopular with those in the galley below.

2 Step-aerobics: This is now a popular sport, and is ideal for a small boat. You must find a step of the right height, though, as stepping on and off a high seat in the cockpit can lead to torn ligaments and damaged muscles. If you have an inflatable dinghy, you will find that when fully inflated it is just about right; you can step on and off it, and with practice you should develop a rhythmic bouncing movement. When you are bouncing with confidence you could try some *trampoline exercises* on your inflatable – but be careful not to spring too high, in case you get out of control and get caught on the rigging, or bounce over-board.

3 Skipping: This is excellent exercise for those of us who are light and nimble – but again could give the deck too much of a hammering if you tend to be on the plump side. On the plus side, there are plenty of ropes on board, of lengths and weights to suit all abilities. You could tie the end of one to something rigid, and ask your partner to turn the other end; then you can skip in and out. Keeping unhooked from cleats and winches will certainly help your reflexes.

Do encourage your partner to have a try. Most men haven't done this sort of skipping before, and they can find it quite exhil-arating – so mind he doesn't get over-excited and jump too hard in one spot. We always have to take care not to damage our superstructure.

4 Gymnastics: This activity could be the answer for some people. It is not so easy in a confined space; but if the boom can hold your weight, you could use that for bar exercises. Do take care, though, not to do any vaulting, as it would be all too easy to misjudge a spring and disappear over the side. If your partner is game, why not involve him in some gymnastic manoeuvres? You could try a few lifts together – but again, take care if you stand on his shoulders, as there is always a chance that he could become unbalanced and topple you over the side, or down the hatch. (You might think I'm being over-cautious, but I can assure you I speak from experience.)

5 Ballroom dancing: This is an excellent form of exercise, especially for the more mature sailor. My husband bought a tape once in a second-hand shop in Burnham on Crouch. It was Part Two of Music for Romance, and as he played it on the boat we relaxed to the rhythms of the bossa nova and samba. I thought then how pleasant it would be to change after dinner into evening dress, and glide out through our canopy into the cock-pit to dance under the stars. We could restrict our movements, and dance on the spot together; we could whirl round in a Viennese waltz, or do an old-fashioned tango. The only thing that stops us having a go is the fear that my chiffon gown will get caught up in my husband's new tackle.

6 Archery: This is an excellent exercise if you need to stand in one spot, but it could be a little hazardous to other boats – espe-cially in a crowded marina. If someone could invent arrows for adults like children's ones, with rubber suction tips, the risk of injury would be reduced. But having shot these safety arrows as a child, I can't remember them ever sticking to the target, so most of them would get lost at sea.

7 Clay-pigeon shooting: Although this sport also requires only a small area for the participant, I fear it would be even more unpopular than archery. As well as being noisy, the bits of clay pot would rain down on people's heads as they tried to relax. It should be possible to alter the equipment, and have rounds of polystyrene pulled aloft, and a gun that shot them down with corks – but even a cork can be painful when it falls on you from a height.

Field and track events

1 Throwing: I wouldn't recommend a hammer or javelin, but you can throw a bucket or a danbuoy – and if you are particularly well muscled in the upper torso, you could try 'shot-putting' a mooring buoy. (Remember to unshackle it from its chain first.) One of the best things to throw is the fender. Having lost a few this way, I've tried tying a length of strong elastic to the end – then when it's in the air you can give it a sharp tug, and it will come winging back. There is a knack in catching it, though, as you have to duck to avoid being twanged by the elastic; and if you're not careful the fender will zoom straight past you, and possibly land on someone else's boat – involving you in the inconvenience of having to ask for it back.

If, like me, you suffer from giddiness when you twirl around throwing things, you can wear a life-line to keep you on deck, but this can restrict you from spinning freely, and can cause you to throw prematurely.

2 Pole-vaulting: I much prefer this event. The boathook is just the right length for a vaulting pole; and if you plant it firmly on the floor of the cockpit, you can attempt to clear the boom. Try running on the spot before you vault to get a bit of momentum. This also loosens the knee joints. (Sadly, I've had to give up vaulting the boom and jump on to the cockpit lockers instead, as I suffered some painful jarring when my pole got jammed in the wooden grating on the floor.)

3 Hurdling: I've already mentioned running on the spot, but occasionally you can get a longer run when you're moored

Keeping fit

Bunk exercises

Hurling the Fender

Introducing your partner to skipping

alongside other boats. Then you can try something more exciting. If you run across all the decks, you can hurdle the rails as you go. As you pick up speed you should be able to clear most of them. Your aim should be to cross all the decks between you and the shore without tripping up.

I find it pays to 'walk the course' first, to judge the height of the rails and the spaces between the boats. Take note of any obstacles, like washing pegged out, as this could hinder your progress. And have a really close look at the drop from the end boat on to the pontoon – many promising hurdlers have been lost by misjudging the gap.

It is also good manners to warn other boat-users of your intentions before you start. When you have made all of these preparations you can set off with confidence, your athletic figure gracefully clearing each rail, landing lightly, regaining balance then off again – a kind of shipshape Sally Gunwhale.

I hope next time you go sailing you will try out some of these ideas; but when all's said and done, probably the best exercises are those you can do sitting or lying down on your bunk. You can stretch most of the muscles in your body if you concentrate hard and use your imagination. I have found, for example, that when I lie on my bunk I can put my feet on the ceiling; and pushing gently I can exercise my upper thighs, lower knees and calves. I also find that from my bunk I can reach out to accept a mug of tea, and this stretches the muscles in my arms and shoulders. A good time to practise is when the washing-up needs to be done.

After you've limbered up and shivered your timbers, and shown a leg or two, your body should be in much better shipshape. To get it to conform to Bristol fashion it must be trim, but also, just as important, it must be clean. For gone are the days when it was thought to be macho to wear the same pair of underpants for a fortnight. Although the experts say that man's biological perfumes are nature's way of attracting a mate, I must admit that I for one don't find the whiff of body odours in any way alluring.

I'm sure we all slip up in this department at some time when on board, so here are a few suggestions on how to avoid giving offence to your fellow sailors. Some of the language used is fairly explicit, so if you are of an ultra-sensitive disposition, you might prefer to skip this section and move on to the following chapter, where you will find nothing offensive.

Using your heads

Relieving yourself on board can be a stressful, if not distressing, experience – especially if you are on a small boat in mixed company. Women are definitely at a disadvantage, and it's only when they go sailing that they realise there are advantages to having a bit of plumbing that is flexible enough to be pointed over the side of a boat.

Women, on the other hand, have to expose so much of themselves, and aren't able to aim with any hope of accuracy. You soon learn on a boat that privacy is an ideal state that is desired but rarely attained. You can try to be discreet, but modesty is just about impossible in such confined quarters; and it's often difficult to perform natural functions without making noises. The perpetrator usually thinks that they can be heard by everyone on board. This can lead to a reticence to let rip, and in some cases can result in irregular motions, or even severe constipation.

One incident that occurred when sailing with friends illustrates this situation very well. After a few days at sea, during which trips ashore had been restricted, we two women were keenly anticipating our visit to the Ladies at the marina, with its attendant promise of relief (necessitated by two consecutive meals of mixed bean salad). As a rule, we co-ordinate the menu more carefully; this duplication was unusual and unfortunate. So it was that with girlish excitement that we tripped ashore, eagerly clutching our loo rolls.

The Ladies loos were in a long marble-clad room, with acoustics second only to the Royal Festival Hall. Our footsteps rang as the door locks clanged; and as the echoes of our chatter resounded from the tiles, we considerately chose cubicles at either end of the deserted room. We sat expectantly, but the silence was oppressive. Suddenly the stillness was shattered by an ear-splitting breaking of wind – from her or from me, or both, we'll never know – followed by shrieks of laughter, bordering on hysteria. I for one was unable to achieve anything after that, and having washed our hands we set off back to the boat.

Our husbands watched us approach with solemn interest; they said they could hear us laughing from the other side of the marina. What was the joke, they asked? We were too hysterical to tell; and later, when we'd calmed down, we felt they wouldn't really appreciate the nuances of the situation.

Yet there is always something to be gained from every experience, and we can all learn from each other's mistakes. This incident shows how important it is to plan a balanced diet; and, if possible, to avoid cavernous public conveniences if you feel you might cause distress and alarm to other members of the community. However, on a more positive note, the story does show that when you're cruising you have to make your own entertainment – and it's surprising how easily you can be amused by quite simple diversions.

Safety note: There are particular hazards associated with relieving oneself during a storm. If you 'use the heads' (Boatspeak for going to the loo), do take care how you position yourself. One unfortunate chap I once sailed with, who was gallant enough not to 'go over the side' in front of someone to whom he'd only recently been introduced, went below in a heavy swell. Standing in front of the sea-loo, and no doubt having raised the seat in a gentlemanly manner, he was suddenly catapulted forwards, and crashed violently on to the seat. Not surprisingly, he caused considerable damage to the seacock.

Later, our Skipper instructed us in the proper toilet safety procedure, and stressed how important it was to turn and sit firmly on the seat in rough weather. This sounds a simple enough action, but anyone who's tried it will know how hard it is to carry it out – especially if you have nine layers of clothing to negotiate.

Performing your ablutions

Washing one's body on a boat is rarely a simple affair, unless you are fortunate enough to have enough space to turn around freely. In most boats you are restricted in the amount of body surface you can physically reach, although in a choppy sea you may find that when being uplifted by a wave you can wash parts that are normally inaccessible.

Usually, washing on a boat of average size is but a cursory affair. Most marinas have good showers; but as with most activities connected with sailing, it is a good idea to plan ahead to avoid some of the problems that can arise. The aim, as always, is to try to maintain civilised behaviour. It is so easy to lower one's standards – one must be very careful not to let things slip.

And it's certainly very easy to let things slip when having a shower in a marina. Apart from letting slip the occasional expletive when the shower sprays needles of icy water on your head, the soap can all too easily slip out of your grasp. You leave the shower that's now blissfully hot, bend down to retrieve the soap from the corner where it lurks, and immediately the hot water turns to icy ramrods that pepper your buttocks. You then leap up to turn off the water, and manage to flick the towel off its hook on to the watery floor, where the sodden thing lies in a soaking wet heap at your feet.

Showering without tears

Here are a few tips to help you:

1 It's sometimes very disappointing when you arrive at the showers carrying all your gear to find that the door is locked. After a few days at sea you will be feeling rather sensitive, but don't take it personally. Track down the person in charge, and you should be given a key, sometimes with a secret combination that will be whispered in your ear. It's worth writing the number somewhere on your person – there's bound to be some salt-encrusted area you could scratch it on.

2 For some reason many outside doors to showers are very stiff, and tend to clang shut unexpectedly once you're inside. If this happens, you can suddenly be plunged into darkness, groping desperately for the light switch. 'Is there anybody there?' you cry, but your voice echoes unheard in the empty blackness. Keep calm. STAY BY THE DOOR TILL YOU HAVE FOUND THE SWITCH. If you wander off to explore in the dark, you could accidentally tumble into a shower cubicle – or even experience the unnerving sensation of being blown on by an automatic hand-drier. But you'll be safe by the door. You can always open it a chink to let the daylight in to locate the switch.

3 Check you've got everything with you before you get undressed. When at last you've got inside a shower cubicle, there's such a feeling of relief that it's all too easy to relax and take all your clothes off. Only then when you take out all your familiar washing bits and pieces, and look for somewhere to put them, do you realise with horror that there's some vital object missing. It's usually the soap, or shampoo, or even the towel.

*If possible, try the shower
before you stand under it.*

If the men's showers are next door and you think your partner might be in there, you can call through the wall and ask to
borrow his soap/shampoo/towel. You can often hear the men
splashing about and laughing. (What do they do in there? Are
the men's showers the same as the women's, or are they all
soaking in a communal tub singing bawdy songs?) As soon as
you call out, there will be total silence. They will all have stopped
splashing to listen. Who is that woman panicking next door?
Your partner will probably be too embarrassed to respond.
Sometimes if you persist in calling out, a strange man will
answer. You should then check the door to make sure your cubicle is locked, and try to manage without the soap/shampoo/
towel.

4 If possible, try the shower before you stand under it. This is
not always easy to do, as some showers are impossible to turn
on at a distance. In this case, make sure you take your clothes

off first, then brace yourself for the initial extremes of temperature. It's wise not to grab hold of the top of the partition and swing yourself up out of the way of the water – the tiles can be slippery, and there's probably someone in the adjoining cubicle with a dicky heart. The last thing you want is to have to resuscitate her when you've both got nothing on.

5 In some showers you have to press a knob to keep the water flowing. This is straightforward until you want to wash your hair, when you need both your hands. If you have a high pain threshold you can try leaning on the knob, or if you are flexible it is possible to use your knee or your foot, though I wouldn't recommend this unless you are in the peak of condition (see the section on Exercises at the beginning of this chapter).

WARNING: *On no account try anything gymnastic without first locating the soap.*

6 If your shower compartment has curtains, be careful how you move about. Curtains around showers, as in shop changing rooms, are never quite big enough. Also, for some reason (possibly static electricity), plastic curtains seem to be attracted to wet bodies, and if you get close to them and turn suddenly they will wrap themselves around you like a piece of clingfilm round a chunk of cheese. Because of this clingfilm effect, you should never bend down to pick something up from the cubicle floor with your back to the curtain. It will mould itself to your body, and as you stand up, you will whisk it to one side. Just at this moment someone will be standing holding open that outside door (probably trying to find the light switch), attracting the wolf whistles of a boat-load of French yachtsmen.

7 Drying your hair can be a problem. You have to improvise with what you can find. Occasionally there are warm air machines, though there are so many machines nowadays you can't always tell one from another. You may be unfortunate enough to put 20p in the slot and your head underneath, only to have a Tampax drop on to your head. Some hand driers have an optional blowing position so that you can direct warm air towards your hair. If the hot air only blows downwards, you can still dry your hair as long as you're under 3 feet tall.

If you remember these tips you will have a reasonable chance of emerging from the shower cleaner and drier than when you went in. Yet I sometimes dream of simpler and kinder ways to clean the weary mariner – perhaps something a bit like a car wash, but sized down to fit a person. If only you could step on to a conveyor belt and have soft fluffy brushes move around you, while warm water sprinkled you gently and soft soapsuds perfumed your body... but what if the machine broke down? Would you be caught up in it, imprisoned until an attendant was called to let you out? And where would your clothes be? What if the machine was set for a tall person, and you found yourself smothered in the brushes?

These are the things that nightmares are made of! Best to stick to the tried and tested methods. At least they're reasonably safe and non-threatening... now, has anyone seen the soap?

8

Oneupwomanship

The following paragraphs are taken from a book called *The British Male Order Catalogue*, by Desirée Morrison, the well-known zoologist. She has made it her life's work to study British Man from every angle, and this book is concerned with his tribal behaviour. This excerpt is particularly relevant to us, as Desirée gives an account of the time she spent living with the sub-species called Nautical Man:

'The British Male as a species', writes Desirée, 'is certainly a rewarding subject for the serious student. I have been studying him for years, and there are still aspects of his behaviour that I find fascinating. We know that the sub-species Nautical Man converses in an ancient and eccentric language, Boatspeak, and practises a variety of rituals, many of which are still only partially understood.

'I was privileged not long ago to be able to spend a week in close contact with a small group of the species Nautical Man, and was able to live as one of their tribe, or "Crew", in one of their floating dwellings. I shared the rather cramped and primitive living quarters they choose to inhabit, and ate the same food as them. I made every effort to communicate with this most endearing creature, so often misunderstood by those who do not take the trouble to study him in his natural environment. By the end of the week they nearly accepted me as one of them, and I was almost sorry to have to go, to return to "normal" civilised society.

'I made some interesting discoveries during my stay. I particularly wanted to make a study of Nautical Man's display behaviour, and the curious rituals associated with it. You might think that such an advanced species would have outgrown the need for competitive display, and at first sight this would seem to be the case; for there is nothing in their outward appearance to suggest that the males were trying to attract attention to themselves, such as the gaudy plumage that is so apparent in the male of many birds and fishes. Indeed, the dress worn by the tribe could only be described as drab. Most of them seemed to favour a uniform navy-blue, occasionally brightened by an orange or yellow covering, or a colourful head-piece.

'As a result it is not immediately obvious which of the group is dominant, in contrast to other animals such as the gorilla, where the muscular physique of the Silver-Back sets him apart from his fellows. Among the tribe of Nautical Man you will not see members of the group displaying brilliant colours on their bodies or prominent crests on their heads; you will not see them making threatening gestures with bared teeth, or beating their chests to affirm their dominance. I did once see two males crashing their heads together, and my immediate thought was that this was a trial of strength, such as you see between two stags; but I soon realised that the clash had been accidental, caused by the two men trying to grab the marmalade at the same time. The appeasing gestures each made to the other after this incident made it clear that there was no rivalry involved.

'However, I did come to discover that although the display and dominance rituals were not immediately apparent, there was certainly a dominant male, whose authority was accepted by all the other Crew members, and indeed there were subtle distinctions between them all that were fascinating to observe.

'I noticed first of all that although the physique of the dominant male was in no way superior to the others, he was able to enforce his authority by his tone of voice. He spoke loudly and curtly at certain times, and this led to an instant response from the Crew – who rushed around to carry out his orders. He also practised certain rituals, such as listening to the radio, at specific times of the day. These rituals were very important to him, and if he overlooked them he would immediately chastise the particular member of the tribe whose duty it was to remind him.

'I also noticed that once they'd released their boat-home from its moorings, and it was "under way" (Boatspeak for "sailing along"), the Dominant Male would frequently look up to the top of the mast, then he'd look at the sails, then his eyes would go back again up the mast. I took this ritualised lifting and bowing of the head to be a form of prayer. Since it was usually followed by instructions to the Crew, I assumed that this was his way of receiving inspired guidance.

'I was interested to see that the Dominant Male had certain pieces of equipment that set him apart from the others, like charts and tools that he used in his calculations. These he kept in a special place, and if they went missing he raised his voice even louder, so that the rest of the tribe scurried around until the tools had been found.

'Occasionally the tribal Crew tried to achieve dominance, or enhance their status in the eyes of the Skipper. This was usually done in a peaceful manner; the aim was to attract the attention of the Dominant Male by doing something that was considered particularly bold and daring. This could be a deed of endurance, like taking the tiller during a gale and guiding the boat safely through the storm. The physical changes that resulted – the frozen hands and blue nose, combined with numb toes and involuntary movements of the lower limbs – were admired appreciatively, and seemed to be an essential part of some kind of initiation test. There were other actions, some involving spectacular leaps from boat to shore, or particularly skilful manoeuvring of the boat, that resulted in admiration and increased status.

'I also found that when the tribe was gathered at a quiet time when the boat was moored, they liked to carry out another kind of ritual behaviour, in which those who might not have performed great deeds could mimic the actions of those who had. This was done in the form of stories. I compared this to the action of some animals and insects, who mimic the appearance or behaviour of other more poisonous or powerful creatures, and in so doing escape being eaten themselves.

'In the evening gathering of the Nautical Tribe, one of the tribesmen would begin by relating a story about some deed or achievement of his own; this would then be taken up by another member of the Crew, who would do his best in a competitive manner to outdo the first man's account; his story would show how he did an even braver thing, or travelled further, or conquered more females of the Nautical Tribe or other tribes. And so they would take turns, vying with each other for status within the group.

'Occasionally the Crew member whose turn it was to speak was unable to outdo the last speaker; I soon learnt to interpret

Two men from the Nautical Tribe displaying competitive behaviour

the physical signs that revealed his obvious distress. I noticed the quiet mood and anxious expression; a knitting of the brows and gritting of the teeth indicated his increased tension. Sometimes in this stressful situation, where an individual was unable to outdo the others by tales of achievement, he would tell a tale in which he'd done a foolish thing; this often caused the others to laugh heartily, thus relieving the tension. In this way, the Crew member would achieve status by his ability to amuse his fellows.

'Indeed, humour played a large part in the culture of the Nautical Tribe. Rather than tell stories, they used at times to tell what they called "jokes", which often resulted in them all laughing loudly, and stamping their feet, or thumping the table. This too was a competitive activity, and there was some rivalry in which crew members, and even the Dominant Male, would attempt a joke of mammoth proportions, which if skilfully done would enthrall his listeners and produce gales of mirth; but if done by a less practised teller, could cause yawns, grimaces, or even cries of derision.

'There are many other devices by which the members of the

tribe maintain the structure of their group, while at the same time allowing for individuals to challenge the Dominant Male in a largely ineffectual way. I was fortunate in being presented with the opportunity of passing one kind of initiation test, as one of the tribe with whom I was sailing was laid low by seasickness – a surprise to us all, as only the night before he'd been telling us that he'd circumnavigated the globe several times without any apparent ill-effect; but as a result of his sickness I was asked to take his place at the tiller. The weather was wild and cold, with bitter winds and high seas.

'When we finally reached our destination, I realised with pride that I had achieved the Frozen Hands of Fortitude, as well as the Blue Nose of Endurance. The other Crew members noticed these marks as they prised my fingers off the tiller. After that, their attitude towards me changed. They began to speak to me almost as if I were an equal!'

I find these words of Desirée very heartening. It shows that we *can* become members of the Tribe – yet it wasn't easy for Desirée, and it won't be any different for you and me.

But we don't all want to be left till the end when the Tribal Leader picks his team. How can we catch his eye? How can we get him to say, 'Who *is* that fantastic woman? Did you see what she did? I can't wait to have her on my side.' If you want to raise your profile, increase your street cred and be one of the boys, it's worth considering doing something spectacular – perhaps one of those Bold and Daring deeds that so impressed Nautical Man.

There are several to choose from, but one of the best crowd-pullers is Going up the Mast. If you decide to stage this event, make sure you publicise it well beforehand. Pin up some posters, and send out fliers to neighbouring boats with just enough details to tantalise, such as:

Don't miss this amazing event!
Rosalind Upshot ('Climbing Rose') attempts to scale the mast!
Tea and biscuits in the cabin after the ascent

When the big day comes, aim for style; choose something eye-catching to wear. A glittery leotard looks very glamorous, worn with fishnet tights and a shiny cape. Try to dress your partner in a matching outfit; after all, he is going to be hauling you up, and will be in the spotlight too. So how about tights and satin trunks for him? If you can't find what you want, just improvise. It's surprising how you can transform a swimming costume with a few glittery bits of foil, or try sewing metal washers and nuts on to your partner's trunks. If you have a fishing-line, those spinning fishing lures can be eye-catching when sewn on in strategic places, as can the feathery ones. (Mind you take the hooks off first!)

Instead of tights, make do with thermal underwear under your costume. It's surprising what you can get away with if you have poise; stand erect with a theatrical pose, throwing your cape around you (the storm jib is ideal for this), and you are bound to impress. Now decide how you are going to make the climb. If you can, shin up the mast with only a safety line. This looks exciting, but is really only for the very athletic. Most women would prefer to have some support, like a sling or a plank of wood. Best of all is the bosun's chair, but this is not terribly flattering to wear, and will conceal the lower half of your costume. A word of warning here – if you do opt for the bosun's chair, make sure you don't put both legs in one hole. This will put you off balance, as well as looking ungainly.

When you and your partner are ready, and while the audience is settling down, do a few limbering-up exercises. A couple of hand-springs will get their attention, or a cartwheel or two around the deck. This looks professional, as well as helping to control shaking legs and hands.

Once you are ready, with your safety line and any other aids to climbing securely in place, toss aside your cape and indicate to your partner that you are ready to make the ascent. Aim to make the climb look both elegant and exciting. Pause now and again to rest, and unhitch your tights if they get caught on the shrouds; then pose by stretching out a leg or two before moving on up.

If you are feeling confident, stop by the spreaders, swing yourself across, and do a couple of gymnastic movements, hanging by your hands, or upside-down with your knees over the spreaders. This is bound to get some applause from the crowd.

However, this sort of display does depend on the weather. If it's windy you'll find it much more difficult to let go of the mast.

*Sometimes it helps
to show off a bit.*

When the whole boat starts to swing, relax, and go with the movement. Try to sway with style, keeping your gestures elegant. At this height you won't hear the gasps of the crowd, but remember that their admiring eyes will be fastened on you.

Eventually you'll reach the top. You will probably feel elated at this stage, but resist the temptation to climb up and stand on the top of the mast and acknowledge the cheers of the crowd – just wave regally, and prepare for the descent. Coming down is comparatively easy, as long as you take it steady; but you still have to be on your toes. 'There's many a slip twixt the mast and the ship' as they say, and your aim is to make a smooth descent. Watch out for the last bit when you might come down too fast and land in a crouched position, which can look rather undignified; or you might find that with a cautious hauler you could be suspended for some time, reaching vainly for a foothold. Also, beware of straddling the boom. This can be more of a shock than you might think, when your nerves are already on edge.

When your feet finally hit the deck you should be greeted with rapturous applause. Respond with a bow and a wave (don't forget to acknowledge your partner), then skip lightly away to get changed and put the kettle on. But do check that you've disentangled yourself from all the lines first! You don't want to ruin the effect of your performance by running to the hatch, only to be pulled back again by the safety line; nor do you want to catch your toe in a stray warp.

Once the crowd has dispersed, and you've done the washing-up, the excitement will fade and a feeling of anti-climax will creep over you. But as you unpick the washers and nuts and drop them into the tool-box, and fasten the spinning lures back on the fishing line, think back with pride on your moment of glory, when you made a bid to become a member of one of the world's ancient and glorious tribes. For already you have become part of a legend. In years to come people will sit around their heaters and tell the story of the day they saw Climbing Rose go up the mast…a spectacular feat of Oneupwomanship.

9

●●●●●●●●

The Tender Trap

Do you sometimes feel that the thrill of romance has gone out of your sailing? That sometimes, when you have been confined with your partner for hours, or days, or weeks, and the rain is pouring down, and you've looked up the answers to all the clues in the crossword puzzle book, life begins to lose some of its sparkle? That you even start to get on each other's nerves? You look back wistfully to the times when you would meet your partner unexpectedly on the far side of the deck, and you'd greet each other with a loving embrace. Or you recall the evenings when you wanted nothing more than to gaze into each other's eyes over your mugs of soup.

There are many, many causes of stress and disagreement, and tensions can build up until something snaps. If it's not your backstays, it could be something more serious, like your nerves. At times like this you can feel as if you're a prisoner on your own boat. You need to do something drastic. It's not enough to zip yourself up in your sleeping-bag; to preserve your sanity, you will have to escape.

But how to get away? You are moored a hundred yards from the shore. Think of all the different ways you could get from boat to land. Dig a tunnel? Your boat might feel like Colditz, but this is not the best way – it's far too time-consuming. Or shooting a line of string from a bow, and aiming for the nearest tree? Yet if you've replaced your arrows with rubber suction tips (see the section on archery in Chapter 7, 'Shipshape and Bristol Fashion'), your arrow is unlikely to stick to anything – and even if it did, the line might not hold your weight.

Build a raft? You could tie fenders together, or save empty lemonade bottles. But where would you conceal it? Your partner would be bound to find it sooner or later. Or swimming? You might make it to the shore, but you'll have trouble taking your bag with you. You could put the bag in the dinghy, and pull it along with the painter in your teeth, but do you have sufficient confidence in your teeth? Or you could climb into the dinghy and row ashore. On the face of it, this is the most sensible solution. But would you be able to do it?

This is where we have to face the brutal truth: we are prisoners on our boats. Unless we can row the dinghy we can never escape! But why can't we do it? I have a theory about this. In fact, it's a conspiracy theory: I *know* that once upon a time women were able to row, but that *THEY HAVE BEEN PREVENTED FROM DOING IT – BY MEN.*

What evidence do I have, you may ask?

1 There is written evidence. A whole section of Boatspeak words and phrases has been censored and expunged from the textbook; this is the vocabulary that refers to women rowers, or 'Rowladies' (pronounced 'Rolladies'). More of this later.

2 There is an oral tradition – a number of rowing songs and rhymes that clearly show how women used to excel at this activity.

3 Archaeological evidence, such as graffiti scratched in caves, and shreds of women's underwear caught in coracles, shows that women were rowing from very early times.

So why did they stop? The simple answer is: because they got too good at it! They were able to row fast and in all directions, often away from their men – hence the men stopped them. These men suppressed the terminology, and they forbade the singing of rowing songs. They destroyed the light coracles (or 'tenders' as the women called them, reflecting their affection for their little craft); and they made dinghies that were too heavy for women, with oars that were too long.

You may have noticed that there was a short-lived revival of the old customs in the mid nineteenth century. Women began to recall and record some of the rowing songs and legends, and there grew up a lively feminist movement, the Rowladies' League, with the aim of restoring the right of women to row. The supporters of the cause were rather militant, and were led by Melanie Bratwurst, who despite her Germanic name was fiercely British in her outlook. She is chiefly remembered today for her design of a practical rowing outfit for women, similar to cycling bloomers, called 'Knicker-wursts'. These garments allowed

Melanie Bratwurst in her rowing outfit

Veil- tied under chin to keep
hat on in windy weather

Back and front stays
to keep the Rowlady erect

Knee-length
Knickerwursts

Flexible hose

Brown &
beige pumps

Original 'wurst'-shape
rowing knickers

women to step in and out of dinghies without the restrictions of
their long skirts.

Sadly, although she rallied the support of many women (and
some men), Mrs Bratwurst failed to win over the powerful men
of her day. She also antagonised Queen Victoria by chaining herself to the Royal Yacht. The Queen was heard to say that she
'couldn't fathom the woman out'. However, Victoria was later
glimpsed wearing a pair of tartan Knicker-wursts, and the
Rowladies' League viewed this as giving a form of royal assent
to their cause.

So why not pick up the banner dropped by Mrs Bratwurst and her band? We should seize the opportunity to re-learn this ancient skill. If only we could handle the dinghy, the world would be our oyster; we would be free to come and go as we please, and if we have to go for good, at least we now have a means of escape.

By now you will be convinced that you should master this skill. But before you take the oars, first let's consider some of the problems that you might come across in the early stages of learning.

Getting in and out

Many people have trouble getting in and out of dinghies, and this is because they aren't sure where their centre of gravity is. It's really not as difficult as you might think – it's all a matter of weight and balance.

Try to imagine that you are rigid, lying horizontally, and being supported by a stand – perhaps something rather like a bird-bath. Where would the stand have to be placed to get you to balance?

You can conduct a few simple experiments to test your answer. See how far you can lean without falling over; or if you have an athletic partner, you can try something more adventurous. Ask him to lie on his back and lift you in the air with his feet. Hold on tightly to his hands and stretch out straight (Fig. 1). You will find your centre of gravity at the point of balance, or fulcrum, where your partner's feet are supporting you.

Fig 1

Conclusion: Your centre of gravity will depend on your shape. Most people find their centre of gravity is around the hip/stomach area, depending on how much excess weight they carry above or below the waist.

For example, a very busty lady would have a higher centre of gravity than a pot-bellied man (Fig. 2).

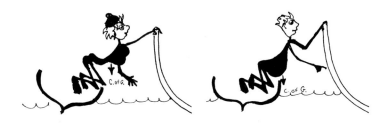

Fig 2

To put this into practice: when getting into a dinghy, aim to put your centre of gravity safely in the middle of it as soon as possible. If you have a large bust, don't lean over the edge. If you have a vast bottom, keep low in the boat – and don't sit too close to the gunwhales. And we all know you shouldn't stand up and wave your arms around, even if you are surprised by something wet or prickly on your seat.

Yet stepping from a sailing boat into a dinghy is an even more hazardous manoeuvre. There is a real danger of the descending person either doing the splits (Fig. 3), or else stepping into the dinghy but leaning on to the boat for support, so that a very unbalanced position results (Fig. 4). Prompt action is required here, and the dinghy must be brought sharply towards the boat before you let go of *anything*.

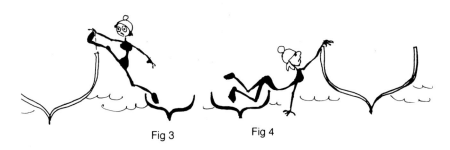

Fig 3   Fig 4

Learning to row

The following rowing terms are taken from a sailing manual of about 1930. These are in the original feminine Boatspeak, and this is one of the few remaining books where they have survived uncensored. To help you learn some of these unfamiliar words and phrases, I have tried to clarify the instructions by including simple diagrams.

The position

In Fig. 5 you will see that the person rowing, the 'Rowlady', (pronounced 'Rollady'), has her oars, or 'rowpoles' (pronounced 'ropples'), too far down in the water. In other words, her rowpoles ('ropples') are *lying a-deep the ding* (or dinghy). In fact, the Rowlady ('Rollady') is *placing low*, or *delving for dabs*. It's a wonder her rowpoles are still in their rowlocks (pronounced 'rollocks').

In Fig. 6 another (less sturdy) Rowlady is making the opposite mistake; here her rowpoles are too far out of the water, and she will be making a bit of a splash. Her *rowpoles are lying light-long the ding*, and she's *placing high*, or *catching crabs*. Not only will she not make much progress, but her companions will get spattered with spray.

In Fig. 7 we see the ideal position; the Rowlady is sitting comfortably, and *making good the ding*.

Fig 5

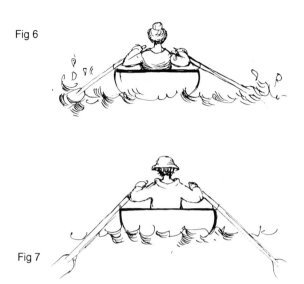

Fig 6

Fig 7

Steering the dinghy

This is a problem for many beginners. Varying the pull, or heave, on the rowpoles can result in dramatic and often unexpected changes of direction. In these views 'from the crow's nest', as it were, you can see how different amounts of energy exerted on the rowpoles can change the direction of the ding.

In Fig. 8 the Rowlady is going straight, or 'even-heaving'. In Fig. 9 the Rowlady is turning to starboard, by rowpoling (pronounced 'roppling') on the port rowpole ('roppling on the port ropple'). In Fig 10. the rowlady is turning to port, by rowpoling on the starboard rowpole ('starboard ropple').

Too much pull on one rowpole can lead to a circling movement, which results in *twirling the ding*; you've probably heard the cry 'Watch out! The ding's a-twirl!' – to which the reply could well be, 'It's all right, I'm just turning to', which indicates that the Rowlady is doing a deliberate rotation.

In Fig. 11 you can see what happens when the Rowlady expends a great deal of energy, while at the same time letting her rowpoles get out of position; if they come free of the rowlocks she can suddenly become unbalanced and fall backwards. Known as *back-toppling*, it can be most embarrassing.

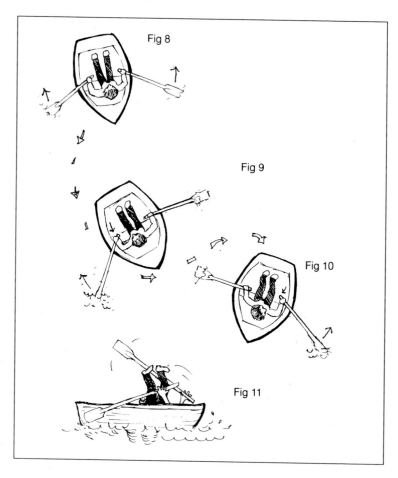

Fig 8

Fig 9

Fig 10

Fig 11

The ability to *heave* on one rowpole while pushing on the other, or holding it down in the water, comes only after lots of practice. If you manage to keep the ding steady, you are said to be *wind-breaking*, or *fluting*. When you have mastered this technique, you will be able to control your twirling.

Leverage

It helps when you're rowpoling to have something to rest your feet against. Rowladies (Rolladies) are often at a disadvantage because in general their legs are shorter than men's, and they are often lacking a pushing platform, or *planking foot*. If you

82

have your partner in the dinghy with you, ask him to sit opposite you so you can put your feet on his, or against his shins or knees, depending on how amenable he is. In this action you are *extending your pins* while your partner is *knuckling under*. (Note: *Knuckling under* is one of many seafaring terms that has come into everyday usage. To 'knuckle down' or 'knuckle under' nowadays means to brace yourself for some unpleasant or demanding activity. 'Knuckle duster' was originally a piece of cloth kept by a man to protect his trousers or shoes when a lady put her feet on him.)

Once you get the hang of it, rowing can be an exhilarating experience. At one time it was quite a social event, and the women would have sung songs as they rowed along in convoy. One woman would begin, and her neighbours would take up the refrain. Sometimes they went on for ages. Here is a selection of rowing songs, both old and new, with a few explanatory notes, where necessary:

ROW YOUR DING

Row, row, row your ding
Round and round all day;
Rollicking, bollocking,
Roppling, toppling,
Tumbling in the bay.

Unfortunately, some of the words that crop up in these old rhymes have now changed their meaning (eg bollocking – or 'bowlocking' – was originally a word used to describe the movement caused by the bows rising up and smacking down in a stormy sea – hence the warning cry 'bowlocks!' when the violent motion tipped up things below decks). Because the word came to be considered offensive, the rhyme fell into disuse.

A WOMAN WENT ROWING

A woman went rowing one day after tea;
Doverly solo, haricots vers –
For to visit her aunt who lived over the sea;
Betty-go-lightly, allons sur la mer.

The waves they grew high and the ding it did fill;
Doverly solo, haricots vers –
'Watch out!' cried the woman, 'I'm feeling quite ill!'
Betty-go-lightly, allons sur la mer.

The water crashed in, such a violent flood!
Doverly solo, haricots vers –
She baled and she bucketed hard as she could.
Betty-go-lightly, allons sur la mer.

'Can you help me?' she called as three seagulls flew past;
Doverly solo, haricots vers –
'Just throw us a line! We'll help you go fast.'
Betty-go-lightly, allons sur la mer.

As you might guess from the mixture of French and English, this
song dates from the period of the Napoleonic Wars. It has a
steady rocking rhythm, which makes it an ideal rowing song,
and it has many more verses, so that the Rowladies could keep
heaving on their rowpoles as they all sang together. (If you want
to know the end of the story, the seagulls pulled on the line
thrown by the woman, and brought her across the Channel. She
never did reach her aunt, though, as she met a gallant
Frenchman and they had numerous adventures together. The
verses were often improvised, according to the skill and imagination of the women.)

Our next song brings us right up to date. It is a plaintive little
number that was popular in the late 1950s, and it shows how
persistent is the attachment that women feel towards their ding,
or tender:

LOVE MY TENDER
Love my tender
Love my ding
Keeping fit that way.
To September
From the Spring
Roppling all the day.

Love my tender
Love my ding
Guess I always will.
Like a seagull on the wing,
Roppling up the rill.

Finally, there is the 'Ladies' Liberty Dance', which was very popular before it was banned. This song became the rallying cry of the Rowladies' League, and was usually performed, with actions, at their conventions. Even in these liberated days of lycra and elastic the words still have power to move us, showing as they do how these pioneer rowladies suffered from the restrictions of their underwear – their backstays griping up, petticoats luffing, and their thick stockings hanging in a cringle. So like the rowladies of old, let us throw off all restraints, and row even-heaving into the sunset, fluting with carefree abandon as we go.

LADIES' LIBERTY DANCE

1 Come, girls, we're dancing in a ring
Unlace your corsets and hear the whalebones ping!
Twirl them round your head and toss them in the air –
We are the Rowladies and we don't care.

CHORUS
Take 'em off, take 'em off, everybody cries
Unlace your corsets and hurl them to the skies.

2 Come, girls, we're dancing round and round,
Shake off your petticoats and drop them on the ground!
Lift up those knees and make the people stare –
We are the Rowladies and we don't care.

CHORUS
Take 'em off, take 'em off, everybody cries
Shake off your petticoats and hurl them to the skies.

3 Come girls, we're dancing in and out,
Off with your baggy drawers and hear the people shout!
Skip around the circle, leap o'er every pair –
We are the Rowladies and we don't care!

CHORUS
Take 'em off, take 'em off, everybody cries,
Off with your baggy drawers and hurl them to the skies!

FINAL VERSE
Come girls, we're dancing in the nude!
Don't you think we're naughty, don't you think we're rude?
Nobody can stop us! Catch us if you dare –
We are the Rowladies and we don't care!

• • • • • • • • •

Making Waves

What better way to end than with a story? This one hasn't been told for a long, long time. In fact, I stumbled upon it quite by chance when I was in the library, trying to find details of the Rowladies' League. The librarian had just gone up the ladder to look for the biography of Melanie Bratwurst. I knew she'd be a long time, so while she was trundling up and down the shelves I took a copy of Coleridge's poems from the shelf, and looked for the 'Rime of the Ancient Mariner', one of my favourites. The book was very dusty; I held it by the covers and shook it, and out dropped an old sheet of parchment.

The writing on it was in some ancient language unknown to me, but the librarian said it was an early form of Boatspeak. We found an expert who was able to translate it, and to my excitement it turned out to be a story from *Bullrush's Almanac*, the sacred book of the Nautical Tribe.

The story tells how the first sailing couple in the world were made; in fact, it's a tribal creation myth, and would have been told by the ancient Nautical Men as they sat round the fires in their primitive marinas. So here is the story of Madam and Steve:

'In the beginning, the Lord of All Sailing made little boats to float upon the face of the waters. He caused his winds to blow gently upon them, and they moved slowly across the waters of the Fairweather Sea.

'Then he said, "I will make living people to sit in these boats that I have made." He made a female person, and then he made a male. The female he called Madam, and the male he called Steve. One pair made he, and set them in one of his little boats, and they were carried hither and thither upon the face of the deep.

'Then spake the Lord unto them, "Lo, I have given thee all things whereof thou mightest have need. I have given thee a boat for thy home, and all the fish that leapest in the sea for thy food. But one command give I unto thee. Many provisions have I provided, and all are good; but of the biscuit that is in the galley thou mayest not eat. For that is the biscuit of the knowledge of Seamanship, of which thou art forbidden to learn, lest thou gettest above thyself, and strive to become like unto the Lord of All Sailing."

'And so the boat drifted upon the Fairweather Sea for many days. The sun shone, and the fish leapt into the boat, and Madam and Steve sat in their cockpit and caught them; yet nevertheless they were discontented. Then spake Madam unto Steve, "What shall we do? I am weary of preparing these fish for thee."

'Then went the man Steve below, and saw the biscuit whereof the Lord had said "Eat thou not of it." And in the biscuit lodged a weevil. Now the weevil was an evil weevil, and did tempt the man. "Come, eat," said the weevil. "Too much fish is bad for thy health; the biscuit is as sweet as the honeycomb and it will give thee an abundance of energy."

'Then Steve was tempted. He brake off a fragment of the biscuit and did eat. He called to Madam, "Come below, and eat with me." When Madam saw what Steve had done she was afraid, but Steve prevailed upon her, saying "Thou art my mate; we are in the same boat, and whatsoever I do, so must thou do also." Then the twain did eat, and at once their eyes were opened. They saw that they knew not where they were, nor whither they were going.

'So they took the flags with which they were clothed and tried to make a sail. The Lord of All Sailing was sitting in his boat in the heat of the day; he heard them disputing one with the other, and he looked and behold, they were lifting the sail aloft to catch the wind. He was sore annoyed.

'"What hast thou done?" quoth he. "Hast thou eaten of the biscuit whereof I forbade thee to eat?"

'Thus spake Madam, "The man gave it to me, and I did eat." And Steve said, "It was not I; the weevil that lodges in the biscuit, he tempted me, and I did eat."

'Then spake the Lord to the woman, "Cursed art thou, O Madam. Because thou tookest the biscuit from the man, and

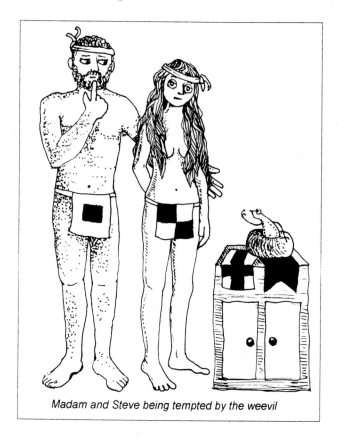

Madam and Steve being tempted by the weevil

didst not think for thyself, thou shalt henceforth be called Crew;
thou shalt have knowledge, but no one will listen to thee. Thy
place shall be down below, in the galley."

'And to Steve he said, "And thou, O man, cursed shalt thou
be. Because thou wast tempted and didst give in I shall cause
my winds to blow upon thee, and my rains to wet thee, and
thou shalt strain to lift and pull. Thou shalt be called Skipper, and
thou shalt have no rest from ceaseless command. Even so thy
Crew will not heed thy word."

'Then spake the Lord to the weevil, "And thou, O weevil, art
most evil of all the weevils that lodge within biscuits. Thou and
thy offspring will lose the power of speech; thou shalt be
knocked from thy biscuit and man will crush thee between his
fingers."

'Then the Lord of All Sailing caused a great storm to arise, and it troubled the face of the deep. The winds blew Madam and Steve in their boat west of the Fairweather Sea into the rough oceans, and they were tossed upon the waves. The sail was ripped and the provisions were scattered about the galley. Everything was in confusion, and there was no longer peace in the boat.'

This is all that was written on the fragment, and the ending is rather sad. Madam and Steve have lost their paradise, the Fairweather Sea. You can tell that the future is going to be hard for them. Still, it's only a story, made up by the Nautical Tribe to explain why there is discord between men and women when they go sailing.

Nowadays we know better. Science has given us ways to cope with our problems. Men who suffer from the Change at Sea can take tablets, we have waterproof clothes to wear instead of flags, and our increased knowledge of health and hygiene has eradicated pests like weevils from our boats.

So one day we shall have made our own paradise on earth. We shall all be fitted with electronic communication devices in our brains, so we shall understand each other perfectly without even needing to talk, and our boats will be so cunningly designed that they will be sailed by computers. We won't need to shout instructions to each other, or argue about where we're going. We shall just sit quietly in our cockpits, waiting for the fish to jump.

And yet...isn't there something missing? A quarrel perhaps, or a little misunderstanding or two – something to give a pinch of spice to sailing? I'm not sure if I want eternal harmony. Like Madam and Steve, I'd rather take the biscuit, venture out on the Great Voyage of Life, be buffeted by the storms and enjoy the lulls, and have the fun of trying to understand my partner all over again...

Index